SCREW IT, LET'S DO IT.
EXPANDED

SCREW IT, LET'S DO IT. EXPANDED

Lessons in Life and Business

Richard Branson

First published in Great Britain in 2007 by
Virgin Books Ltd
Thames Wharf Studios
Rainville Road
London
W6 9HA

A catalogue record for this book is available from the
British Library.

ISBN 978 0 7535 1149 7

The paper used in this book is a natural, recyclable product
made from wood grown in sustainable forests. The
manufacturing process conforms to the regulations of the
country of origin.

Typeset by TW Typesetting, Plymouth, Devon
Printed and bound in Great Britain by
CPI Bookmarque, Croydon, CR0 4TD

CONTENTS

PREFACE: THE BIGGER PICTURE

I was first invited to write *Screw It, Let's Do It* for World Book Day 2006. The idea was to offer something enjoyable and inspirational to emergent readers that would encourage them to pick up books and read more.

The first edition of my little book did far better than I ever dreamed it would. It sold all around the world, reaching No. 1 in South Africa as well as the bestseller list in Australia. I was enormously gratified by the degree of enthusiasm with which it was received. Many people wrote to me saying how much the book had encouraged and inspired them. I also discovered that it had reached out far beyond the emergent readers for whom it had been written.

A year on, I was asked if I'd like to write a revised and expanded version for a wider readership. In this new version of *Screw It, Let's Do It*, you will find all my original lessons in life as well as new ones that look to the future.

Though I have never followed the rules, at every step I learned many lessons along the way. They began at home when I was young. They continued at school and in business, when I ran *Student* magazine in my teens. I am still learning and hope I never stop. These lessons have held me in good stead throughout my life and I hope that you will find something in these pages that might inspire you.

Newspapers call my partners and me at Virgin 'Mavericks in Paradise' – perhaps because I own two idyllic tropical islands; one in the Caribbean and one off the coast of northern Australia. There's no doubt that we tend to do things in a less stuffy way than most businesses, and for me, it works. I work hard and I play hard. I believe in goals. It's never a bad thing to have a dream, but always I'm practical about it. I don't fantasise and sit daydreaming about the impossible. I set goals and then work out how to achieve them. Anything I want to do in life I want to do well and not half-heartedly. At school, I found reading and writing hard. Back then, dyslexia wasn't understood and my teachers thought I was lazy. So I taught myself to learn things by heart. Now I have a very good memory. It has become one of my best tools in business.

We have come a very long way since I launched Virgin back in 1967. We started small and grew big. Sometimes the pace of our expansion into numerous fields and enterprises, from cola, to wine, wedding gowns to mobile phones, books, comics, animation, credit cards, planes, trains and even space travel, seems incredible. Nothing seems impossible or too big to tackle. Virgin really does wholeheartedly embrace my maxim 'Screw It, Let's Do It', and I love to see the enthusiasm and energy generated by our team. I relish it when we take on a new idea and make it fly.

But we are now into the new millennium and the old ideas that industry is king and the devil take the hindmost are changing. With huge leaps in science and our understanding of the way the Earth and the Universe work, we have come to realise that everything is linked; nothing stands alone or acts on its own. For every act there is a consequence. Because of this, I feel it is very important to know how Virgin is going to work in the twenty-first century.

On a global level, the behaviour of people, industries and enterprises has immediate and often long-term effects on our world. If mankind makes a mistake, it can be catastrophic. On a personal level, Virgin employs over 50,000 people, and their livelihoods will be affected if we don't succeed in all the many areas we have established ourselves. As a businessman, of course, I want to get on and be successful, and sometimes the cheaper option in manufacturing methods seems the better one. But one of my rules is: *Do no harm.*

It seems to me that, along with my responsibility as chairman of one of the world's most successful and entrepreneurial companies, I have a responsibility and duty, as much as is humanly possible, to ensure that we do no harm. I have taken to heart the fact that everything we do touches something, or someone, somewhere.

For a long time I have been drawn to the Gaia Theory, a hypothesis formulated by James Lovelock almost forty years ago, which states that the Earth is a living entity, like a single cell, and, like a single cell, everything it needs for its existence is contained within it. Moreover, Professor Lovelock believes that the planet can heal itself if damaged. But even with Gaia there is a point of no return, beyond which the damage could be irreversible. Environmental scientists have warned us that the pace of development and industry, as well as the loss of vast tracts of rainforest, has released so much CO_2 into the atmosphere we have entered into a cycle of global warming which could lead to the destruction of most forms of life on Earth. This is happening *now*. We must put the environment first if we are to survive.

As a capitalist I faced a stark question: was I doing harm? Careful research and investigation revealed that there was a way in which I could be a capitalist and still embrace my long-held environmental philosophy. By looking at ways in which Virgin could develop new fuels to reduce carbon emissions, we could help to reverse global warming. We could also take steps to make our group of companies more environmentally responsible. I coined the phrase 'Gaia Capitalism' as a tenet, a catchy phrase, and as a way forward.

I have come to realise that while industry and enterprise exist on a wide-scale commercial level, they don't have to be bad. Of course we all want to have refrigerators, drive cars, hop on planes and trains, live our normal, busy and satisfying lives. But at the same time, we must be more aware of how our actions damage our environment. I believe that it is up to big companies like Virgin to lead the way with a holistic approach, one which, while creating and maintaining successful, entrepreneurial companies, also helps maintain the balance of nature and does as little harm as possible.

Virgin can do this because we are a private company. I don't believe in going by the book. I will change things where I can if it's for the better and I will work by setting an example. In this I have been influenced by many good and brilliant people. As well as James Lovelock, I draw inspiration from the ideas of my relative, Sir Peter Scott, who set up the World Wildlife Fund before his death; Jonathon Porritt, co-founder of Forum for the Future (and Founder of Greenpeace); Australian scientist and environmentalist, Tim Flannery, who says in his groundbreaking book, *The Weathermakers*, that we can all influence the global climate in a positive way; and Al Gore, who has made it his mission through his film and book, *An Inconvenient Truth*, to get the message across that the world is on the brink of an environmental catastrophe.

My new goal in life is to work at reducing carbon emissions. This is why in Virgin over the coming months and years, we will be looking at every scientific advance, every development – and perhaps offering a few ourselves – that will make for a more organic and holistic approach to business. The future is exciting. We could be on the threshold of a Renaissance not only of the way we all live but also of enterprise and invention.

Related to this, Virgin Unite was set up as a charitable foundation to support a network of grass roots charities that make a difference on both local and global levels. We encourage our staff and customers to get involved, to volunteer, and in this way we are making a difference in many areas, particularly in helping with really tough problems, like malaria, AIDS, HIV and TB.

Education is a key element of this and Virgin has always worked hard for charity and to help the young through Virgin Unite, but I want us to get more involved in innovative ideas where education is concerned. I have already founded a School of Enterprise at South Africa's CIBA University; and will develop a travelling international university with a tented campus. I believe also that we need less politicising and more wisdom, so a key element of my way forward is to establish a Council of Elders, who will offer advice when asked by world leaders. I am honoured that Nelson Mandela has agreed to be the founding father.

When I was starting out in life, things were more certain. You had a career lined up, often the same one your father followed. Most mothers of course stayed at home. Today nothing is sure; life can be one long struggle. People have to decide on priorities if they want to get anywhere. The best lesson I learned was to *just do it*. Whatever it is, however hard and daunting it might seem, as that ancient Greek, Plato, said, 'The beginning is the most important part of any work,' while the Chinese say, 'A journey of a thousand miles begins with a single step.'

If you look ahead to the end, and all the miles between, with all the dangers you might face, you might never take that first step. Whatever it is you want to achieve in life, if you don't make the effort, you won't reach your goal.

Take that first step. There will be many challenges. You might get a few knock-backs – but in the end, you will make it.

Good luck!

Richard Branson

1. JUST DO IT!

Believe it can be done
Have goals
Live life to the full
Never give up
Prepare well
Have faith in yourself
Try and try again
Help each other

When I first discovered that my nickname among some members of staff at Virgin was 'Dr Yes', I was amused. Obviously, it had come about because my automatic response to a question, a request, or a problem is more likely to be positive than negative. I have always tried to find reasons to do something if it seems like a good idea, than not to do it.

My motto really is: 'Screw it – just do it!'

I know many people say 'no', or 'let me think about it', as an almost Pavlovian response when asked a question, whether it's about something small and insignificant or big and revolutionary. Perhaps they are over-cautious, or suspicious of new ideas, or simply, need time to think. But that's not my way of going about things. If something is a good idea, my way is to say 'Yes, I'll consider it' – and then to work out how to make it happen. Of course, I don't say yes to everything. But what is worse: making the occasional mistake or having a closed mind and missing opportunities?

I believe in using and harnessing other people's knowledge and experience, which is why I like to work holistically, within a team. Harnessing energy is like harnessing brainpower. What's the point of selecting someone for a particular task if you ignore his or her experience and ability? It's like consulting experts and not even considering their advice.

I also trust my own instinct and ability to do almost anything I set my mind to. If an idea or project is good and worthwhile, if it's humanly possible I'll always consider it seriously, even if I have never done it, or thought about it, before. I will never say, 'I can't do this because I don't know how to.' I'll ask people, look into it, find a way. Looking, listening, learning – these are things we should do all our lives, not just at school.

Then there are those silly little rules that someone has invented for baffling reasons. I always think that if you set up quangos or committees, they will find something useless to do. The world is full of red tape, created by committees with too much time and an overbearing desire for control. Most red tape is a tangled mess of utterly useless, nonsensical jargon. If I want to do something worthwhile – or even just for fun – I won't let silly rules stop me. I will find a legal way around rules and give it a go. I tell my staff, 'If you want to do it, just do it.' That way, we all benefit. The staff's work and ideas are valued, they feel good about themselves and Virgin gains from their input and drive. People generally don't leave their jobs through lack of pay – they leave because they aren't valued. Many companies put their people in boxes – if you are a switchboard operator, you are always a switchboard operator. But we value our people and encourage them to be adaptable and innovative.

If you recognise something is a good idea, or if there's something in your personal life that you want to do, but aren't immediately sure how to achieve your goal, I don't believe that that little word '*can't*' should stop you. If you don't have the right experience to reach your goal, go in another direction, look for a different way in. There's always a solution to the most complex problem. If you want to fly, get down to the airfield at the age of sixteen and make the tea. Keep your eyes open. Look and learn. You don't have to go to art school to be a fashion designer. Join a fashion company and push a broom. Work your way up.

My mum, Eve, is a perfect example of this. When the war started, she wanted to be a pilot. She was so determined that, despite the fact that she had never learned to fly, she knew she could and would do it. Instead of brooding and dreaming, she went to Heston airfield, close to where she lived, and asked for a job to get her foot on the ladder. On asking what her chances of flying were, she was told only men could be pilots. This didn't deter her – in fact, if anything, she looked on it as a challenge. She got one of the instructors on her side and he told her to disguise herself as a man. Mum was very pretty and had been a dancer on stage, so it was obvious that she didn't *look* like a man, but audaciously, she got hold of a leather flying jacket, hid her blonde hair under a leather helmet and practised speaking with a deep voice. And she got the job she wanted – as she knew she would. All it had taken was ingenuity and grit. She learned how to glide and began to teach the new pilots. These were the young men who flew fighter planes in the Battle of Britain. Later, she became a Wren and helped service the boats that carried troops to France. Modern girls like my mum played a huge role in the war as intelligence agents, munitions workers, in the armed forces or the land army. All of them rolled up their sleeves and got on with what needed to be done.

After the war, airlines were a new business opportunity and Mum decided she wanted to be an air hostess as a means of seeing the world. But back then, air hostesses had to speak Spanish and be trained as nurses. Again, Mum didn't let the rules and red tape stop her. She chatted up the night porter at British South American Airways, a fledgling airline that operated Lancasters and Yorks between London and South America, and he secretly put her name on the list. These planes were the first passenger jet planes, so history was being made. Soon, she was an air hostess. She still couldn't speak Spanish and wasn't a nurse, but she had used her wits to achieve her goal. She just did it. Interestingly, those early passenger planes carried only a handful of passengers, 13 in the Lancaster and 21 in the York, and there was probably more of a sense of camaraderie during the long flights. You also had to be quite brave to fly to remote places. The planes were unpressurised, fragile boxes and oxygen masks had to be worn over the Andes. A year later, BOAC (British Overseas Airways Corporation) took over BSAA and Mum switched to the Bermuda run in Tudor aircraft. The first exploded; Mum was in the second one; the third disappeared in the Bermuda Triangle. The Tudors were grounded, but she continued to fly until she married my dad – a young barrister – who proposed to her while they were bombing along on his motorbike during one of her leaves.

Mum wasn't the only person in our family who said, 'Let's do it!'

The famous explorer Captain Robert Scott was my grandfather's cousin. A man of great courage, he made two trips to the Antarctic as a step in his goal of being the first man to the South Pole. Travelling to either one of the Poles was always an incredibly risky and daring venture in those early years because there was no special equipment, no lightweight, insulated clothing – in fact, bizarre as it sounds, Polar explorers wore their everyday winter clothing, but piled on the layers. Some of them even wore ordinary hats and woollen mittens. Given the high degree of failure – and failure meant certain death – people insisted it couldn't be done. Scott said, 'I can do it' – and he did. He reached the South Pole in 1912, but, because he had delayed until the weather was milder, for the sake of his pack ponies and sledge dogs, he was second. Roald Amundsen, who took only dogs and left in the depth of the Polar winter, was the first. It was a terrible blow for Scott. Worn out and ill, he and his men died on the return journey. Yes, he had made the first balloon flight over Antarctica – an amazing and highly dangerous feat – but people don't remember that. They just say, poor old Scott, he was brave, but lost the race. Winning gives you a buzz, but people shouldn't be embarrassed if they don't come first. Having a go is the important thing, and even if you come second, third or fourth, you'll know that you did your best.

I'm going to spend some time outlining my first real commercial project – *Student* magazine – because I believe my methodology was good and, I also believe, a good example of 'just doing it'. I started *Student* when I was fifteen years old and still at Stowe, the boarding school I went to. I didn't do it to make money – I did it because I wanted to edit a magazine. I didn't like the way I was being taught at school, or what was going on in the world, and I wanted to put it right. A big reason for starting the magazine was to have a platform to protest against the escalation of the Vietnam War. Large numbers of US combat troops began to arrive in Vietnam in 1965 under President Lyndon B. Johnson, and we were reading of aerial bombing campaigns of cities and roads in North Vietnam. Chemical defoliants were also indiscriminately sprayed from the air. It seemed pointless and wrong.

Like many other fledgling entrepreneurs, I didn't see my idea as 'business' but as a politically motivated, though fun, creative enterprise. To me, businessmen worked in the City, smoked fat cigars, and wore pinstriped suits. It didn't occur to me that businessmen could come in all shapes and sizes and backgrounds because, until then, they mostly followed the expected formula. I'd already had some early forays into making money with trying to sell rabbits, budgerigars and Christmas trees (more on those later). Where *Student* was concerned, there was a high degree of trial and error in my efforts; but then, I was only a schoolboy. However, almost instinctively, I followed the basic financial rules of preparing a sound business plan. Charles Dickens' character Mr Micawber in *David Copperfield* had it right when he said, 'Annual Income £20. Annual Expenditure £19-19s-6d, Result Happiness! Annual Income £20. Annual Expenditure £20-0s-6d, Result Misery!' Thanks to my parents' careful juggling with money as we were growing up I knew that income had to exceed outgoings. Profit should be the one and only commercial raison d'être in business, however much fun and enjoyment you get from it. An unprofitable business is a headache, a source of stress, and fiscal madness.

When I told friends and acquaintances that I intended to produce a proper magazine for sale on a professional, commercial scale, and asked for advice and journalistic contributions, I was confronted with some degree of disbelief, scepticism and even hoots of laughter. They treated my project like just another schoolboy enthusiasm. One or two shrugged and said I was too young and had no experience. But I was serious – I really believed in myself, believed it could be done and wanted to prove them wrong. I've always been stubborn and, if anything, their negativity strengthened my resolve and made me all the more determined.

For someone who wasn't all that academic, I had the contrary ambition of becoming a journalist when

I left school. I wanted to travel the world, interviewing people and filing my stories. 'Foreign correspondent' had a romantic ring to it. Obviously, I was a bit young and inexperienced to actually be a foreign correspondent – so instead I got the idea of publishing a magazine. At Stowe, we already had our own school magazine, *The Stoic*, but we couldn't publish dissident and revolutionary thoughts in it – for example, rants against fagging, beatings, compulsory chapel, Latin and all those traditions that every schoolboy in Britain hated or resented, and this is why I got the idea of producing a kind of renegade magazine. It wasn't a wild leap from planning one just for Stowe to deciding that *all* the sixth formers in England would want a copy. I got my schoolmate, Jonny Gems, involved as my co-conspirator and we decided that it would have a wider appeal if we solicited articles from students at other schools and got a forum going. We were convinced that such a magazine would make waves and change the way things had been done for centuries.

I got out a notebook and started to jot down a few thoughts, starting with some ideas for titles first. *Today, 1966, Focus!, Modern Britain, Interview*. It was a bold start. I then listed the kind of articles I wanted to publish that I thought would inspire my readers. The next step was to work out distribution, circulation and costs. In the school library, instead of doing my prep, I went through *Who's Who*, and made a list of 250 MPs, and then made a similar list of possible advertisers by carefully scouring the telephone directory. I wrote everything down in my lined notebook, including my philosophy and the format. The philosophy paragraph read:

A new political magazine with the aim of getting every public school boy more interested in politics and to know about the improvements and 'goings on' at every other public school in the country. Contributors would include other schoolboys, members of the public and MPs.

I started a fresh page, at the top of which I wrote: *Letters to write* and underlined it. Beneath, I wrote, '300 public school masters: $3 \times 300 = 600d$'. (This was for stamps on letters to ask for permission to sell the magazine at their schools. A 'd' was an old penny of which there were 240 to a pound.) Under that, I wrote, 'envelopes, writing paper, 300d. Total, 75 shillings = £3.17.6d' (or £3.75 in modern money). By the time I had finished my sums: 1,000 copies printed to be sold at 1/6 (7.5p), postage, and commission to shops, I was staring at a deficit.

It didn't take us long to work out that overheads and anticipated sales in such a limited circulation area didn't add up. We'd have gone bust before we even started; not a very auspicious start to my entrepreneurial aspirations. Back to the drawing board.

For days, I walked around, deep in thought; or scoured as many newspapers and magazines as I could. What was going on in the world, what was the buzz? I didn't realise it, but instinctively I was doing market research and examining demographics in the most elementary way. Almost accidentally, I had stumbled on a truism: whatever you sell, first identify your market. I think that was when it dawned on me that I was thinking too small. Students were everywhere – and student power was a newly invented phrase that had grabbed the media's attention. *Eureka!* I had the magic bullet.

Changing the name to *Student* instantly widened the field and gave us target sales not only of every sixth former – our original market – but of technical college and university students: hundreds and thousands of potential customers. It was a dazzling prospect and our excitement grew. Now we could offer huge circulation figures to potential advertisers, and also to contributors. We could sell through mainstream magazine wholesalers and retailers, like WH Smith. Instead of saying that a thousand sixth formers might read our little magazine, we would sound convincing when we pitched the giddy premise of twenty, thirty, forty thousand to the money men. In the days before the Internet, it was difficult to find out how many students there were. I know how easy the Internet has made life and research for millions, and, despite my initial reservations, I have to admit that I do find myself with the need to tap into it more. However, my idea of market research is more basic: ask somebody who knows. I believe I picked up the telephone and called someone at the Ministry of Education and carefully wrote down the figure.

I thought that my business plan was scientific and sensible – an approach that might have surprised all my detractors, especially my maths and science teachers at school! I did my sums carefully, working out how much the paper and print bill would be. Then I worked out the income from sales and from selling ads. Contributors, I decided, would be glad to offer their services for nothing.

When I discussed my plans with Mum, as always,

she took me seriously. 'What do you need to get started, Ricky?' she asked.

'Enough money for phone calls and letters,' was my prompt response.

Mum had always said you've got to invest a little to make money. She came up trumps by giving me a float of £4.00. In 1966 this was enough for 320 stamps or phone calls at thruppence (1.5p) each. Today, £4.00 will buy you less than 14 first class stamps. Jonny's father put in an order for headed notepaper with: STUDENT – THE MAGAZINE FOR BRITAIN'S YOUTH printed across the top, with the energising symbol of a rising sun.

My request for a telephone in my study at school was turned down by the headmaster, who was, I think, secretly amused. Nevertheless, although my 'office' desk was given over entirely to the magazine, I had to accept having to use a callbox. My voice had broken, so I sounded older than I was, but the difficulty was I couldn't take calls; I was compensated to some extent, though, by discovering that I could make free ones by the simple expedient of telling the operator that the machine had swallowed my money and I'd been disconnected. Happily, operator-connected calls avoided that embarrassing little 'pip-pip-pip' when the coins went in the box, or when your call was up. A bonus was the operator sounded like a secretary: 'I have Mr Branson on the line for you.'

I wasn't the only person using a public callbox to start an empire – forty years ago, half the budding entrepreneurs in London did. You have to remember that this was the Swinging Sixties and things were changing so fast the old guard's head was spinning with the shock of it all. The Beatles, the Stones, Carnaby Street, King's Road – it was a young, vibrant world and commerce didn't want to get left behind. To my astonishment, they took me seriously.

My system was to write out our letters longhand, and then I sent them home to Mum. She got Elizabeth, a friend in the village, to type them out and send them back to me in batches for signing and posting. Jonny and I spent almost two years writing hundreds of letters trying to sell advertising space until I suddenly got the knack of how to sell the sizzle. I'd tell the advertising manager at Lloyds Bank that Barclays were taking the inside back page – did they want the prestigious back page itself before I offered it to the Nat-West? I vied Coca-Cola against Pepsi. I honed my presentation skills, my sales pitch, and never gave a clue that I was a fifteen-year-old schoolboy standing in a cold callbox with a pocketful of pennies. Remarkably, it worked.

Making those phone calls, writing those letters and waiting for the replies was more fun than Latin lessons. I was wildly excited when eventually we got our first cheque from a bank for space. It was £250, a huge amount. Jonny and I walked around for a week, wide grins illuminating our faces, as bright as the sun on our letter paper. Our final total for ad space for our first issue was £2,500 – which would enable us to pay for a print run of 30,000 copies. It seemed an incredible achievement for two sixteen-year-old schoolboys, when the price of an average house was £3,660 and an E-type Jaguar cost £1,867.

We tried to get content to match our aspirations. Mum pitched in enthusiastically, writing articles, asking her friends if they knew people who knew people. I remember how excited we were when Gerald Scarfe – our first contributor – said he would draw a cartoon for us and be interviewed. I also tried to get interviews with famous people by cutting school and catching the train to London, somehow simultaneously fitting in these extra mural activities with my life at school.

By then, I knew I wasn't destined for university or an academic life: I knew I would do better on my own in the world, and was set on my course as an entrepreneur. My parents let me make my own choice. Despite my father's reservations about my plans to curtail my education and not go to university – which he thought would set me up in life – they were behind me, whatever I did. I still have a copy of a letter that I wrote to them explaining how I felt:

> Anything I do in life I want to do well and not half-heartedly. I feel I am doing my best in *Student* – as well as time allows. To me I saw a danger of falling between two stools and still do. Of being a failure in everything I had and having to search for priorities if I am to get anywhere. I am also still only sixteen.

Then I continued, explaining what I did compared with other boys of my age, and concluded with:

> You did not see the world as it is today when you were sixteen. Your career was almost lined up. Today it is one long struggle . . . *Student* is a career like anything else . . . It is a beginning to my life like university or your finals were to yours.

My parents and I have always communicated well – and even today I think communication is the secret to good business as well as good relationships. They got behind me when they read that letter and my father accepted that I wanted to plough a different field from him. They agreed that I could give up all subjects except ancient history, which I enjoyed. So when it came to my final exams, it didn't really feel like cheating when I filled little cards with prompt notes and hid them all over my clothing, in pockets and up my sleeves, and even tucked under my watchstrap.

Exams over, I was ready to launch myself into the world, armed with absolute belief in myself, and knowing that whatever it was I wanted to achieve, it could be done.

I was still only sixteen when I left school and started working full time on *Student*. I had never really been in business before – other than the usual schoolboy schemes of the lemonade stall variety – but I knew enough to know that no man is an island. We all need someone to act as a counterbalance to our weaknesses and work off our strengths. Sometimes it's one person, sometimes it's a team, all of whom bring their unique talents and abilities to the table. Your family is often your network of support – and my advice to a budding entrepreneur would always be: listen to your family, accept their help, don't dismiss them out of hand.

Jonny and I camped out in the dingy basement of his parents' London house. It was wonderful to be young and free and right in the heart of town. We drank beer, had girlfriends and listened to loud music, just like students – but students who didn't have to study. We worked just as hard, though. I got some amazing interviews, with people like James Baldwin, Jean-Paul Sartre, John Lennon, Mick Jagger, Vanessa Redgrave and Dudley Moore. I was so full of confidence I never paused to ask myself why they were willing to let me in through their doors and talk to me face to face, and my confidence must have been catching because very few people turned me down. It helped that in 1966 there were fewer barriers to meeting famous people. Back then, they didn't have secretaries, front offices and PAs to fend off eager young journalists like me. Mostly though, my success came about because I just picked up the phone and wrote letters. We had more 'names' in our pages than some of the top magazines and, curious about what we were achieving, journalists, major stars and well-known intellectuals started dropping by. Life in the basement was glorious chaos, a non-stop party.

But we had a serious side as well. We wanted to send our own reporters out to cover the big issues of the day, like the war in Vietnam and the famine in Biafra, but we had no money. Instead, we thought laterally about how we could do it. If we told newspaper editors that we were sending a sixteen-year-old to some hot spot to get the youth perspective, we thought they might be interested in his perspective. I called the *Daily Mirror* and pitched it to them. They bought the story and paid for Julian Manyon, who was working for us on *Student,* to go to Vietnam. Today, Julian is an award-winning 55-year-old reporter for ITN. We also made the same arrangement for him to report on Biafra for us.

It was a good lesson to observe how, by stretching our ideas through necessity, we actually came up with something innovative and worthwhile, which also brought us a lot of publicity.

We really believed that we were changing things, making important statements and drawing the attention of the public to important events that otherwise might have been ignored. It wasn't all wars and famines though – we tried to balance the magazine by including politics with rock 'n' roll and used student power to make our mark. We even found that, thanks to those interviews with John Lennon and Mick Jagger and others, we were reaching a wider audience – though their names didn't guarantee easy success. Getting known wasn't easy. We couldn't afford advertising to publicise ourselves, so it had to be word of mouth and direct sales.

I worked hard at getting media publicity, which would increase sales. I did so well at convincing journalists on mainstream newspapers that *Student* was hot, that the *Sunday Telegraph* wrote: 'Photographers, journalists, writers from papers throughout the world seem to have fallen over themselves in assisting *Student*, and a massive voluntary distribution organisation has grown throughout schools and universities allowing, perhaps, over half a million students to read the magazine.' The *Daily Telegraph* added: 'It seems probable that *Student*, the glossy publication that has attracted a lot of well-known writers, will become one of the largest circulation magazines in the country.'

This was fantastic publicity, and one of the reasons why I have spent much of my life being happy about promoting myself and Virgin. Advertising, publicity, promotion – call it what you will – works. Even nature puts on a show – flowers, birds, even beetles, display themselves. There is so much competition in the world, that if you have something to sell, no matter what, you have to get it noticed.

Those early days of hard sell were to stand me in good stead. I learned that we all have something we want to sell, whether it's a tangible object like that ubiquitous can of beans or offering our talents for hire. It was no use producing goods or having the best ideas in the universe if they just stayed in your head or stacked up in a corner of your bedroom. When those first 30,000 magazines came from the printer, in bundles tied with string and still smelling of fresh ink, along with our excitement, we faced reality in the shape of real print bills that had to be paid with real money.

I put up fliers, offering students a means of earning money by selling our magazines. They trekked to our door, picked up a bundle to sell in the street or at university and many became our friends, willing to do whatever they could. The idea was to sell them a bundle at half price and they could pocket the profits, but most students were too broke to pay up front and often they never returned with the cash. It didn't matter – we were getting known, the word was spreading.

We were a close-knit team; all of us willing to get out there and get our hands dirty. Even my family turned up on publishing days, willing to help sell magazines. Their enthusiasm swept us along, making it fun. Mum took a big bundle to Speaker's Corner at Hyde Park and sold them there. My sister Lindi and I walked along Oxford Street in the time-honoured way of all hawkers and traders – even Daniel Defoe had sold his broadsheets and pamphlets on the streets – shouting out: 'Read all about it! Only half a crown!'

I was so fired with energy, with being a part of that historic, living breathing capital city, with its long history of charity and commerce, I felt I could achieve anything. I wanted to embrace every experience and help the world to be a better, kinder place.

In those early days of huge print bills, low sales and advertising that had to be fought for every step of the way, money was always in short supply and we often went hungry, or worried about how to pay our phone bill, but it never seemed to matter. Mum would come by with a hamper of food – calling out as she came down the basement steps, 'Red Cross delivery!' and Jonny and I and any helpers we had would fall on it. Another time, Mum found a necklace on the road and handed it in at the police station. In due course, when it wasn't claimed, she got it back, and knowing our dire need for cash, she sold it and gave us the proceeds – £100 – a fortune, which bailed us out from our pressing debts.

Every time a fresh opportunity came, we grabbed it. When it was obvious that our magazines were reaching saturation point, instead of just accepting it, we looked for more ways of making money. We branched out by being the first people to sell cut-price records by mail order – the first advert went in the last edition of *Student*. When a postal strike stopped us, we looked for another way. Our goal became to open record shops but we didn't have enough money. So we found a man who owned a shoe shop in a prime position on Oxford Street and talked him into letting us use his spare space. We needed a name and it was then that Virgin was born. As we sat around tossing ideas for names into the arena, someone said, 'Well, you're virgins at business. What about Virgin?'

I used the lessons I had learned from *Student* and worked hard to promote the opening of that very first Virgin Records shop in Oxford Street. We made it a 'cool' place for students to go by arranging big squashy floor cushions and booths where they could listen to the records before buying them. They wanted to hang out there and told their friends. And one store led to a second and a third. Our system was simple: we looked in person for a busy street where a lot of people walked and we insisted on a three-month holiday from rent. Without that 'free' three months while the shop was establishing itself, we walked away from many good opportunities. Soon, we had Virgin Records shops in almost every big town – and I was still under twenty years old. Cash may have been pouring in fast, but bills were pouring in faster! We had reached that target but I still had more goals – and gradually, over the years, I have achieved them.

I believe in living life to the full. In 1984, when boat builder, Ted Toleman asked me to sponsor a power-boat to win back the Blue Riband for Britain, I agreed at once. The Blue Riband (which included the Hales Trophy) was the prize for the fastest ocean crossing from America to Ireland and to date it had been won by some pretty impressive passenger liners, like Cunard's RMS *Lusitania* (sunk by a German

U-boat in 1915); the elegant French liner, SS *Normandie*; and finally, in 1952, the SS *United States*, with a crossing of three days, ten hours and forty minutes. Then planes took over, and the day of the great passenger liner was over. The Blue Riband was mothballed, apparently in the possession of the Americans for ever – until we decided to challenge it.

However, the *Virgin Atlantic Challenger* wasn't a great liner of 52,000 tons and 240,000 horsepower like SS *United States*. Our boat was a lightweight, 65-foot catamaran with two 2000-horsepower engines, but there wasn't anything in the rules that said we couldn't win with a small vessel. The only requirement was that it carried passengers. I was delighted to be asked along as a member of the four-man crew and trained incredibly hard to get fit enough for the gruelling crossing.

There was only one slight hitch: my future wife, Joan, was eight months pregnant with our second child and I had promised her that I would be there for the birth. We checked the calendar. It seemed that I could make the attempt on the record and be home in time for the birth. However, storms delayed us in New York for three weeks, and when we finally got news that the conditions were just right for the record attempt, I felt I would let down the team if I didn't go.

Having been there for the birth of my first child Holly – something I will never forget – I knew how important it was that I should also be there for the birth of our second child. I asked Joan, 'What shall I do?'

She didn't hesitate. 'Just do it – go,' she said. 'The baby's not due for two weeks. You'll be back before then.' Given that Holly was six weeks premature, I hoped she wasn't being too optimistic.

We set off from America, crashing across the waves in *Virgin Atlantic Challenger*. At the end of the first day, I got the news on the radio that my son, Sam, had been born. I'd broken my pledge, but most importantly we'd had a healthy child. We all whooped with joy and Steve Ridgway, a member of the crew, rustled up a bottle of champagne to toast Joan and my new son. Without any extra shaking from me, the bottle exploded and fizzed everywhere. It was impossible to drink. Holding on to a lifeline, I staggered to the side and threw the bottle overboard, where it bobbed in the wake. Now I had to power on to see Joan, Holly and our baby boy.

The crossing would have won the record comfortably. But as we approached Ireland with only a few hundred miles to go, we hit a ferocious storm. We had been battered solidly for three days, but this was the worst yet. The boat smashed up and down. We held on to our seats and could see nothing. As we approached the Scilly Isles, with only 60 miles left and the Hales Trophy nearly in our hands, we hit a massive wave. A second later there was a shout from Pete Downie, our engineer.

'We're going down. The hull's split right open. Get out fast.'

'Mayday! Mayday! Mayday!' Chay Blyth, another crew member, was on the radio in a flash. '*Virgin Challenger* is sinking. We are abandoning ship. Repeat: we are abandoning ship.'

Within seconds the boat started to go down. The first life raft we inflated snagged on something and ripped open. We had a backup raft which we threw overboard and pulled the ripcord to inflate.

The life raft was like a tiny inflatable coracle with a hooded tent. We huddled together, rocking up and down in the sea like we were on a crazy funfair ride. I was sitting next to the radio, and I picked up the mike. An RAF Nimrod – scrambled by order of Maggie Thatcher herself – had picked up our Mayday. I gave the pilot our position, and he rapidly radioed any ships in the area.

'OK, there are three vessels in the area that are heading towards you,' the pilot came back to me. 'In no particular order, there is the *QE2*, which is heading for New York; an RAF helicopter from the Scilly Isles has been mobilised, and a Geest boat heading to Jamaica is also on its way. Please take the first one that arrives.'

Eventually we were picked up by the Geest banana boat on its way to the Caribbean. We were winched up in turn and left the life raft spinning by itself.

We had failed on the first attempt to win the Blue Riband, but we didn't give in. A year later, I was back with *Virgin Atlantic Challenger II*. The boat was 75-feet long, with a single hull. We were confident that she could cope with the heavy seas much better than her predecessor. We left New York Harbour on a bright June morning and headed up towards Nova Scotia. The trip up the east seaboard of America was much faster than we hoped.

By the second day the adrenaline rush which had kept us going had worn off. It was now just horrible, relentless banging. Each wave smashed us up and down, up and down: we had to just clench our teeth and bear it.

As we were trying to leave our second refuelling boat, our engines coughed, choked, and conked out. Eckie Rastig, our new engineer, went below decks to investigate. He came back up horrified: the fuel filters were full of water. This was a disaster. It was a complete mystery as to how the water had got in with the fuel, but we had no time to worry about that. The diesel and the water had emulsified together, which meant it was impossible to split the water off from the diesel: we had to drain the entire four fuel tanks and start again.

We restarted the engines but they conked out again. We had now spent seven hours bobbing up and down next to the refuelling boat in the middle of the freezing ocean. The race was slipping away. The swell grew progressively worse.

'The storm's catching up with us,' Chay said. 'This isn't funny.'

The storm, which was following the wonderful weather we had enjoyed on the first day, was not an abrupt, fierce storm, but just a big spell of filthy weather, our worst nightmare. Soon the boat was riding waves which had grown to 50 feet. By now the suffocating petrol fumes made us all sick. Everyone was retching and puking and doubled up in pain.

'It's not worth going on,' Chay shouted in my ear. 'We've all spoken and we're all gutted. It's over. I'm sorry, Richard.'

I knew that if we failed on this attempt there would be no third time. We had to go for it. I had to persuade them.

'Let's just try to get the engines going and see how far we can get,' I said. 'Come on. We've got to make a stab at this.'

We all summoned up our strength again and went into action. We cast off from the refuelling boat and, with a bit of fine-tuning, the engines roared back into life. They were coughing and spluttering and liable to cut out, but at least they worked and we didn't have to get out the oars.

We reached the third refuelling ship and, with another set of full tanks and some Irish stew for us, our first hot meal in two days, we approached the last leg of the crossing with rising determination.

When we passed the point where we had sunk on the previous attempt we all cheered and suddenly knew that we could do it. Five miles out from the Scillies, we were met by a posse of helicopters and then hundreds of boats of all kinds who welcomed us home. We had done it. Our total journey had lasted 3 days, 8 hours and 31 minutes: in a voyage of over 3,000 miles, we had beaten the Blue Riband record by a mere 2 hours and 9 minutes. We did it. The lesson I learned from that, and which I live by, is to keep trying and never to give up.

The day after we had won the Blue Riband, a Swede named Per Lindstrand telephoned me. 'If you thought that crossing the Atlantic by boat was impressive, think again. I am planning to build the world's largest hot-air balloon, and I'm planning to fly it in the jet stream at 30,000 feet. I believe that it can cross the Atlantic. Do you want to join me?'

I thought of my old hero, Captain Scott, remembering the stories of how he had flown in a balloon over Antarctica. No one had ever crossed the Atlantic in a balloon before. I had never been in a balloon before. It was mad. It was too risky. By then, my companies were dealing in hundreds of millions of pounds. What would happen if I died? All these thoughts spun through my mind as I listened to Per outlining his plans and why he thought it would work.

There were many sound, sane and solid reasons why I shouldn't go. In fact, there was only one reason why I would even consider going – and that is, I can't resist a challenge. But I had heard of Per Lindstrand and vaguely knew that he held some ballooning records, including one for reaching the highest altitude. This man seemed to know what he was talking about.

'I'll never understand all the science and theory,' I said, 'but I'll come with you if you answer me this one question.'

'Of course,' Per said, stiffening his back in readiness for some incredibly challenging question.

'Do you have any children?'

'Yes, I've got two.'

That was good enough for me – if he would take the challenge, so would I. I shook his hand and said I would join him.

I always tell people that if they want to do anything well, they must plan and prepare. I had trained hard for the Blue Riband record attempt and I knew I would have to put the same amount of preparation into our proposed adventure in a balloon. It was about as risky as it gets. If a ship sinks in the sea, the chances are in your favour that you'll be rescued – but a balloon is totally unpredictable. There's no telling where unknown winds and jet streams will blow it, or where and how fast it will plummet to earth. We were going to fly five times further and keep the balloon up three times longer at a greater height than anyone – including Per – had managed before. The first step was to learn to fly a balloon and to do it so well that I'd obviate as much risk as was humanly possible. So I went to Spain with Per and Robin Batchelor, my instructor (who looked like my double), and learned how to fly a balloon. Those lessons saved my life.

Until you have been in a stratospheric balloon, you can't imagine the sheer size of it compared with the balloons used for advertising or half-hour flights often seen over the countryside. It's like comparing a bicycle with a bus – and it seemed unbelievable that I was contemplating doing what no man had done before, to coin a phrase.

A balloon filled with helium, like the old zeppelins, can stay in the air for several days. A hot-air balloon relies on the hot air within the envelope rising above the surrounding cold air and taking the balloon with it. But the loss of heat through the balloon's envelope is rapid, and, in order to heat the air, balloonists burn propane. Until Per's proposed flight, hot-air balloons had been hampered by the impossible weight of fuel needed to keep them afloat.

We'd save fuel by flying at 200 miles an hour and heating the air in the balloon with solar power during the day; we would have a pressurised capsule instead of a wicker basket – all new methods.

'What will stop stratospheric winds ripping the balloon to shreds?' I asked.

'I've designed a double skin,' was Per's response.

His answers were solid and scientific and I grew more confident that if anyone could succeed, it would be us. Because the winds and the jet stream blow from America to Europe, we left from America very early one morning. Twenty-nine hours later, we were over Ireland, the first people to have crossed the Atlantic in a hot-air balloon.

The incredible speed of our flight gave us an unexpected problem: we still had three full tanks of fuel attached to the capsule, and they could well explode on landing. We decided to swoop down very low and drop off the fuel tanks in an empty field, and then come down a second time for a controlled landing. Per stopped burning propane and brought the balloon down low so that we could see where we could safely jettison the extra fuel tanks. As we came down, the wind suddenly swirled around us, much harder than we expected. The ground rushed up to meet us. Travelling at a speed of almost 30 knots, 35 miles an hour, our groundspeed was not so much the problem as our sudden plunge downward. We hit the ground and bounced along a field. All our fuel tanks were torn off by the impact, along with our radio aerials. Without the weight of the tanks, we hurtled back upward. I didn't see it, but we narrowly missed a house and an electricity pylon.

With no fuel tanks we were utterly out of control. The balloon was rising like a rocket. We saw the coastline approaching and Per vented hot air from the top of the balloon to reduce our height. But once again the ground wind was considerably stronger than we expected and it swept us out to sea. We were heading northeast, and without the radio or electricity in the capsule we were more than ever at the mercy of the wind.

'Hold tight,' Per said.

He let out more air, alternating this with burning propane to try to reduce the speed of our descent through the thick grey cloud. As we finally came out of the fog, I saw the foaming sea rising up to meet us. We'd missed the beach. We were going far too fast.

We hit the sea, crashing me into Per. We were tilted at a crazy angle, unable to stand upright. The balloon started to drag us across the surface of the ocean. We were being bounced from wave to wave.

'Get out!' Per shouted at me. 'Richard, we've got to get out.'

Per braced himself against the hatch, wrenched down the levers and pushed it open. The balloon slowed for a moment as the capsule dug into the water, and Per heaved himself up and climbed through the hatch.

'Where's your life jacket?' I shouted.

Per didn't seem to hear me. He threw himself off the top of the capsule into the cold black water. The drop seemed at least 100 feet. I was sure that he'd killed himself. Without his weight, the balloon shot up fast, too high for me to jump. I was on my own.

I floated higher and higher into the clouds, the winds carrying me north, towards Scotland. I was alone, flying in the biggest balloon ever built, with only about an hour of fuel left. When it went, the balloon, the heavy capsule, and I with it, would plummet into the sea. I tried the radio. It was dead. I had two equally dangerous choices and didn't know which one to go for: I could jump out in my parachute or stay put. It really did seem that I might die. Fatalistically, I got out the notebook I carry everywhere, and wrote, 'Joan, Holly, Sam, I love you.'

Suddenly, my old optimism and determination kicked in. What on earth was I thinking of, giving in without a fight? 'While I'm alive, I can still do something,' I said to myself. 'Something will turn up.'

As the fuel expired, the balloon drifted down through thick clouds. I floated through the bottom layer, towards the grey sea and saw a helicopter skimming above the waves. It was searching for me! When the crew acknowledged that they had spotted me, I knew I would be saved.

Close to the waves, I jumped into the sea, away from the balloon. Without my weight, it flew up and out of sight – but at least I didn't have the anxiety of having it land on top of me. The helicopter fished me out of the icy water and as soon as I was reeled up into safety, I asked about Per. They looked perplexed. 'We thought he was still with you,' they said. All the time I'd been flying northwards with a dead radio, I'd been worried sick about Per. He had been in the sea for hours and we had to find him quickly. I gave them his last position and he was rescued just before he died from exposure.

The whole trip was an amazing experience. I learned many lessons: not only that if you want to do something you should just do it, but also to prepare well, have faith in yourself, help each other and most of all, never give up.

All of these lessons can be used in life. You don't have to run a big business, fly in a balloon, or break records in a boat to learn from and use the lessons I learned. Your goal can be small. *Student* magazine was very small at first. I sold space in it from a payphone at school because I believed I could and would do it. If something is what you really want to do, just do it. Whatever your goal is you will never succeed unless you let go of your fears and fly.

2. HAVE FUN!

Have fun, work hard and money will come
Don't waste time – grab your chances
Have a positive outlook on life
When it's not fun, move on

I have read in various articles that I turn everything I touch into gold. While that's not true, I don't deny that I have done well and have enjoyed a considerable amount of commercial success. Taxi drivers, journalists, radio interviewers, frequently ask what my secret is, how do I make money? What they really want to know is – how can *they* make money? Everyone wants to be a millionaire.

I always tell them the same thing. I have no secret. There are no rules to follow in business. I just work hard and, as I always have done, believe I can do it. Most of all, though, I try to have fun. I sincerely believe that work should be tempered by fun, and by that, I mean enjoying myself, not working and worrying and getting stressed out. I don't see the point of spending every waking moment working, sometimes to the point of exhaustion. Fun refreshes us; it's stimulating and vital on physical and spiritual levels. Knowing how to laugh and love and appreciate each other is what life is about.

The proverb, all work and no play makes Jack a dull boy is a truism that goes back four and a half thousand years to an ancient Egyptian sage, who wrote:

> He who works all day is miserable. He who plays all day doesn't pay his bills. The bowman hits the mark, as the sailor reaches land, by having different skills and knowing when to work and when to relax.

When I was about to go around the world in a hot-air balloon – a venture I knew was very risky and from which I might not return – I wanted to leave my children a small piece of advice from my heart, something I thought would guide them in the years ahead. Before I left, I wrote a letter to Sam and Holly, in which I said, 'Live life to the full. Enjoy every minute of it. Love and look after Mum.'

Those words sum up what I believe in. Don't waste time. Have fun. Love your family.

Notice that making money isn't in that list.

I didn't set out to be rich. The fun and the challenge in life were what I wanted – and still do. I don't deny that money is important. We are not cave men and women who can live on just roots and berries. However much an idealist might resent it, we live in an era when we must have some money to survive. I once said I only need one breakfast, one lunch and one dinner a day, and I still live by those words. I never went into business just to make money – but I have found that if I have fun, the money will come. I often ask myself, is my work fun and does it make me happy? I believe that the answer to that is more important than fame or fortune. If something stops being fun, I ask *why?* If I can't fix it, I stop doing it.

You might ask, how do I know that fun will lead to money? My answer would be that I don't know it – I can only offer myself and my way of living my life as an example. Success doesn't always happen and I have had my downs as well as ups, and of course I don't fritter away every day playing – I'd quickly get bored. Relaxation is good, holidays are important, but I think what I really mean is that we should enjoy what we do, whatever it is. Our work should inspire and satisfy us. We spend so much of our lives working to make a living that doing something we loathe seems pointless. I believe in balance, what Buddhists call harmony. On the whole I have been very lucky maintaining this balance. For almost as long as I can remember, I've had fun and I've made money.

My very first business enterprises, or moneymaking schemes, were not a success, but I learned from them. One Easter holiday, when I was about nine years old and home from prep school, I came up with a great plan. I would grow Christmas trees. Everyone wanted a Christmas tree, so it seemed logical to conclude that quite literally Christmas trees were a cash crop – and what's more, they just grew themselves. Pound signs danced in my eyes. I found out where to get the seedlings and sent away for them. As soon as they arrived, I asked my best friend, Nik Powell, to help me plant some 400 seedlings in our field at home. We worked hard making holes with a gadget called a dibble and dropping in the seedlings, but like all boys who like to mess about on the farm, we also enjoyed ourselves. All we had to do was wait for the seedlings to turn into Christmas trees in eighteen months, sell them and count the money. Even at an early age I planned long term.

The first lesson I learned was how to use maths. I was not good at sums at school. On paper, they were too cerebral and made no sense because I had the kind of mind that needed to visualise figures that had a purpose. As I planned our Christmas tree business I saw at once that if a bag of 400 seedlings cost £5 and each tree sold for £2, we would make £795 in profit. That was real money, worth waiting for.

My second lesson was that money doesn't grow on trees! Sadly, rabbits ate all the seedlings. We got some revenge. I'm sorry to say we had fun shooting the rabbits, which we sold for a shilling each to the local butcher. Overall, we did make a small profit on the original £5 investment and all our friends had rabbit pie. We all – except the rabbits – gained something.

You never know what you'll find on a sunny beach ... On holiday, I found my very own desert island and an airline. It came about accidentally, when I was working hard building up Virgin Music in 1976. Mike Oldfield had already been our first big success with his *Tubular Bells* album in 1973 and we went on to sign up the Sex Pistols, the Human League and Sting, so things were on the up. We were very busy but we all had a great deal of fun. People said things like 'Branson's a lucky devil' to come across a huge hit like *Tubular Bells*, as if I had somehow tripped over it lying in the street like a dropped wallet.

Yes, it was a lucky break, but we were the ones who had recognised it and took the risk. Mike Oldfield had recently played in the West End stage musical *Hair* and was working as a session musician when he played me some tapes of *Tubular Bells*. I thought it had that almost magical sound which comes along very rarely, but when it does, you know it's special. We didn't have a record company, and sent him off to play his tapes to six other companies. All of them turned him down. We liked the sounds so much that we knew it would be successful. So we formed this little company, initially to launch *Tubular Bells*. We knew it could happen, but making it work was hard for a bunch of kids like us. We had to find the money to sign it up and then we had to promote it really hard in an industry that only wanted genre. We had to think outside the box and asking John Peel if he would play the entire album on his show was something which was unheard of and, as far as we knew, no DJ had ever done before. He agreed. It worked, and sales took off.

The next hurdle was that Mike Oldfield was too shy to promote the album, but we didn't give up. Instead, *we found an answer*. Thinking creatively, and somewhat ahead of our time, we made a video and showed it on television. Groups like the Beatles had made music videos, but as promotional tools separate from the big pop shows, like *Top of the Pops*, they were still rather thin on the ground. Our video got a lot of airplay, but a big breakthrough was to get it used as the soundtrack of *The Exorcist*. Sales were massive worldwide. It put Virgin Music on the map almost overnight. But even though we were so successful, we never stopped looking for new sounds and new talent.

I always try to get away from England in the winter. Music, sun and sea make me feel good and the distance from London gives me the space and freedom to think and plan out fresh ideas. That winter, at the end of 1977 my girlfriend Joan and I had split up. I was sad but I like to make the best of things and I felt even more in need of a holiday.

I went to Jamaica, partly as a holiday, but I also intended to look for bands and sign them up, so I took a suitcase filled with money, because Jamaican musicians won't take cheques. During the day, I swam in the warm sea and at night I sat on the beach or dropped in at little clubs and bars, listening to some great reggae bands. When I heard a new kind of music, I immediately sat up and took notice. It was a kind of early rap made by local DJs and radio jocks, who were known as 'toasters', so I was in at the start of something big. Fortunately, I had the cash in my case that enabled me to sign up almost twenty reggae bands and some toasters. We sold lots of records with them; a perfect example of my motto – have fun and the money will come.

I was still in Jamaica when Joan phoned me out of the blue: 'Can you meet me in New York?' she said. We had a happy time in New York City, but the phone didn't stop ringing and we longed to escape to spend some time alone. At a party, someone asked me if I had named Virgin after the Virgin Islands. We had named the company Virgin because at the time we were virgins in business, but I had never been to the Virgin Islands. Suddenly, they sounded like the perfect romantic place for Joan and me.

I had spent all the cash on signing up bands in Jamaica, but I had heard that if you were looking to buy property in the Caribbean you would get a grand tour, free of charge. I phoned an estate agent in the Virgin Islands, telling him that I owned a record company and wanted to buy an island to build a recording studio on it.

Fortunately for our romantic getaway, the agent responded exactly as I hoped he would. 'Please come as our guests. We have lots of lovely islands for sale. We'll show you around.'

Joan and I flew to the Virgin Islands, where we were treated like royalty. A big car met us at the airport and took us to a luxury villa with a swimming pool and an incredible view of the sea. It had everything we wanted, and that night as we swam and gazed up at the starry sky, it was like being in Paradise. I really did think that I could live like that and dreamed of buying an island of my own. The next day a helicopter was waiting to take us on a tour. We skimmed over green palm trees and a blue sea and landed on one lovely island after another, touring fantastic private estates and having a great time. We spun our free holiday out as long as we could, but at last we were running out of islands for sale.

More to spin out the idyll than any real intention of buying an island I knew I couldn't afford, we asked the agent if he had something we hadn't seen.

'Yes, there's one, a real little jewel,' he said. 'It's miles from anywhere and it's quite unspoilt. Its name is Necker.' He said an English lord owned it, a man who had never been there.

An island that was miles from anywhere sounded good on two counts. The first was it was a nice long helicopter flight with plenty of scenery for us to enjoy. The second was we really did like the sound of it. Unspoilt meant that it had not been built on. Perhaps it would be cheap.

At first, island hopping was a game. We didn't mean to buy an island and I couldn't afford one – *yet*. Virgin Music was doing well, and any one of the bands I had signed up could do well, so I didn't entirely discount the idea of buying an island at some stage in the future. But now I was excited. I wanted to own our own place in Paradise. *I had another goal.*

We flew over a clear blue sea and then a coral reef that completely encircled a lagoon and a tiny island, before landing on a white sandy beach edged with palm trees – it was like a classic scene from *Robinson Crusoe*. In the middle of the island was a green hill, which we climbed. The view from the top was worth the effort. We could see in every direction and there was nothing – just us and the blue sea. The shallow lagoon inside the reef was so clear and clean we could see a giant ray swimming lazily along. The agent said turtles laid their eggs on the fringe of the beach and, in the middle of the island, there were two small saltwater lakes and acres of lush, tropical forest. As we watched, a flock of black parrots flew overhead. There were no big villas, no sign of habitation. It was a real desert island. Standing there, gazing out to sea, I was king of all I saw. I fell in love with Necker on the spot.

The agent warned us that there was no fresh water on the island. If we bought it, we would have to make it from the sea.

'Good,' I thought. 'They can't be asking a lot for a desert island with no water and no house.' I asked him the price.

'Three million pounds,' he said.

It was far beyond my reach. 'I can offer £150,000,' I said.

I was offering less than five per cent of the asking price! I was serious but the agent wasn't amused. 'The price is three million pounds,' he repeated, his smile fading.

'Final offer. I can go to £200,000,' I said.

We walked back down that hill and got into the helicopter. We flew back to the villa. Our bags were waiting outside. We had been thrown out. We spent the night in a bed and breakfast in the village and left the next day. It was like being cast out of Paradise.

We spent the rest of our holiday on another island, with none of the luxury lavished upon us so generously when the agent thought we were seriously rich. Our plan was to travel on to Puerto Rico – but when we got to the airport, the flight was cancelled and people were roaming about, looking lost. No one was doing anything. So I did – someone had to. Even though I hadn't a clue what I was really doing, with a great deal of aplomb I chartered a plane for $2,000 and divided that by the number of passengers. It came to $39 a head. I borrowed a blackboard and wrote on it: VIRGIN AIRWAYS. $39 SINGLE FLIGHT TO PUERTO RICO. All the tickets were snapped up by grateful passengers. I managed to get two free tickets out of it and even made a small profit!

The idea for Virgin Airways was born, right in the middle of a holiday, although the actual airline only properly took off when I was sent a business idea some years later. I had never chartered a plane before, but, as with *Tubular Bells* and the Jamaican toasters, I saw and grabbed the chance. Today Virgin Airways flies to 300 places around the world. We have Virgin Atlantic, Virgin Blue in Australia, Virgin Express in Europe, Virgin Nigeria, and, hopefully, Virgin America. And we've gone further than I could ever have dreamed – Virgin Galactic will offer flights into space. Nobody else is doing that. We are ahead of everyone. In 24 years we have gone from renting a plane to space travel.

Back in London with Joan after our holiday, I still had my goal to buy Necker Island. I did some research and found that the owner of the little island was wealthy, but had never been to see it, which is why he had never developed it. I also found that he wanted to sell in a hurry so he could raise £200,000 to build a house in London – the very amount I had offered the agent. It seemed that my offer was meant to be.

The only problem was, I didn't have £200,000, so I was going to have to borrow it from someone. I offered £175,000, which I didn't have either. When it was turned down I left it at that and got on with work. Three months later, I got a call to say the island was mine if I offered £180,000. I was told that, as part of the deal, we had to make the island habitable within five years by building a house and a desalination plant to make fresh drinking water.

This would cost a lot, but I was positive I could find the money somewhere to do it and I agreed to the terms.

I took a loan from the bank and borrowed from my friends and family. So much debt was daunting, but it spurred me on. I promised myself that I would make enough money to pay everyone back and to fulfil the Herculean tasks of building a house and making fresh water – which I achieved. The enterprises I built up, in part to pay for Necker, continued to make money. So while it doesn't have to be buying an island, this is why I can say, have fun and the money will come and in turn so will your goals.

Today, Necker is a lovely place, where all my friends and family gather together to relax and play. The last episode of my TV series, *The Rebel Billionaire*, was filmed there. The camera filmed from the terrace and showed our wonderful view of the sea, the white sandy beach and the palm trees. It was the same view that Joan and I saw from the top of that green hill all those years ago. I had signed up bands in Jamaica and ended up with an airline and an island. It wasn't always easy. But when you have goals and a positive outlook on life, you have something to aim for. Hard work and fun is what life is all about.

As soon as something stops being fun, I think it's time to move on. Life is too short to be unhappy. Waking up stressed and miserable is not a good way to live. I found this out years ago in my working relationship with my oldest friend, Nik Powell.

Nik was with me from the very start of Virgin. I was the ideas person and Nik kept the books in order and handled the money. His main job was to run the Virgin Records stores and, thanks to him, they did very well. When we started the airline, we wanted it to be the best. We sank millions of pounds into it, but our main rival, British Airways, tried to stop us. As the war between us heated up, we needed more and more money. It seemed an endless pit. Virgin Music was wealthy but the airline was eating up the cash and Nik didn't enjoy taking such huge risks – whereas I always remembered what Mum had said when she gave me that initial £4 to start *Student*: 'You've got to invest money to make money.'

Nik's reluctance to risk losing Virgin Music was when we both knew it was time for him to move on. I bought his shares in Virgin from him and was on my own – if I sunk or swam, it would be on my head. In fact, I had done my sums – just as I had with the Christmas trees – and while my early boyish enterprise didn't pan out thanks to a bunch of greedy rabbits, in the case of the airline I had worked out exactly how much I was risking and it was less than one-third of a single year's profit from Virgin Music. It wasn't that much of a gamble, but I thought running an airline would be fun, as it was, and the potential outcome was worth it.

Nik's first love had always been films. He used his profit from Virgin to start Palace Pictures and he made great films, like *The Company of Wolves*, *Mona Lisa* and *The Crying Game*, which won an Oscar. He is still in the film business, still having fun and we are still friends. After a struggle, the airline finally went into profit. If Nik had stayed with Virgin he might have made more money, but he would not have been happy. If we had gone on working together even after the fun was gone, we might not have stayed friends. He made the right choice. This is why I say, never just try to make money. Long-term success, happiness, and satisfaction will never come if profit is the only reason for your enterprise.

I have been lucky. Virgin now has the luxury of a great deal of money behind it. People say I should relax. I could retire, but I ask, 'What would I do?'

They say, 'Paint watercolours. Play golf. Have fun.'

But I am having fun. Fun is at the core of the way I do business. It has been the key to everything from the start and I see no reason to change it.

Not all of us have the money to set up a business, or the luck, or the chances aren't there. Sometimes, you are glad to have a job – any job. So you grab the job in the factory or the store or the call centre. You might hate it, but you try to make the best of things. But is that fun? I would say, do you really have to stay stuck in a rut? Is the job you hate really your only option? Whoever you are, you have other choices. Look around to see what else you can do.

One company that reflects my own ethos is Ben and Jerry's, the ice cream makers based in Vermont. Ben Cohen and Jerry Greenfield were two high school friends who started their company with a $4,000 loan which they used to open their first scoop shop in an abandoned gas station. Business boomed so fast – today their turnover is $150 million – that these two hippies worried they were becoming a cog in a capitalistic machine. Jerry escaped to Arizona, but Ben remained and founded what he called 'Caring Capitalism'.

Ben says, 'Detached from values, money may indeed be the root of all evil, but linked effectively to social purpose, it can be the root of opportunity.' Like Virgin, his stated mission is to do good and not damage the environment. Ben and Jerry's Foundation gives away 7.5 per cent of its pre-tax profits to charity (the average in the US is one per cent). According to Ben, 'Some people believe that Ben and Jerry's has been successful in spite of its strong stand on social and environmental issues. The truth is that it has stood out precisely because it stands for something different in the world.' That something different is to stay true to their roots and using the power of the brand to draw attention to causes such as preserving the Arctic National Wildlife Refuge, supporting family farms and fighting global warming by reducing waste and offsetting 100 per cent of their greenhouse gas emissions. But they still have fun. Walt Freese, their CEO calls himself 'Chief Euphoria Officer'.

As is well known, I rarely use a computer, but I support progress no matter from where it comes. Virgin uses the Web to advertise our wares, from airline tickets, to wines to books to records and electronic goods. If Virgin sells it, it's available at the click of a mouse. The Dot.com world has opened many new doors. There are work and trading opportunities on the Web. It has changed the lives of people with ideas and energy and the stories of the great fortunes that have been built – from Google to YouTube – are well documented. All of them have been built by computer experts with little or no capital, just a good idea and a garage or shed to work from. But even those with little experience can create a successful Internet mail order business. It makes sense to try to be different, rather than compete in a very crowded market.

Anyone can start up a new business from home. You can wash windows, take in ironing or walk dogs. You can be an artist or a writer. You can be a gardener. You can make and sell dolls' houses. Even the Queen sells her farm produce from Windsor and Sandringham on the Web, as does Prince Charles with his Duchy Originals – which at the end of the day are things like jam and shortbread, which anyone can copy and sell online. Anita Roddick made skin cream in her kitchen in Brighton – now Body Shop is a global empire. You can make salad dressing in your garage like Paul Newman. With him it started as a hobby and now it's a big company. (He gives all the profits to charity. So far, he has given away more than $150 million – not bad for a hobby.) Granted, Paul Newman didn't have to worry about funding, but Anita Roddick had little money when she started out, so there are no rules or absolutes. There are dozens of things you can do from home to make money. It could be more fun and lead to a new career you really enjoy.

If you still have to work for a boss at a job you don't like, as almost everyone does at some point, don't moan about it. Have a positive outlook on life and just get on with it. Work hard, earn your pay and make friends. Enjoy the people you come into contact with through your job – and if you are still unhappy, make it instead your goal to divide your private life from your work life. Have fun in your own time, consider that your boss or your company is paying for your fun, and you will feel happier, and enjoy your life and your job more.

3. BE BOLD

Calculate the risks and take them
Believe in yourself
Chase your dreams and goals
Have no regrets
Keep your word

I enjoyed making the TV series in the US, *The Rebel Billionaire*, because I had fun taking myself and a group of young and enterprising men and women through a range of challenges, many of which were straight from James Bond films – though none was impossible. All of these challenges or tests I could perform myself, and were designed to whittle the group down until we were left with the one person with the strongest character and most suited to achieving his or her goals. The final episode had a twist at the end. We all gathered on the terrace at Necker, in my home high above the sea, as I offered the ultimate prize-winner, Shawn Nelson, a cheque for $1 million. There was a catch. He could take the cheque or toss a coin for an even bigger prize. If he lost the toss, he would lose it all. I held out the cheque. He took it and saw the long line of zeros and you could almost see in his eyes how much such a sum meant to him and his business aspirations. Then I took it back and put it in my hip pocket. Instead, I held out a silver coin.

'Which one will it be?' I said. 'The coin or the cheque?'

Life is full of hard choices. Which one would he go for?

Shawn looked shaken. It was a huge gamble. All or nothing. He asked me, 'What would you do, Richard?'

'It's up to you,' I said. I could have told him, 'I take risks, but they are calculated risks. I weigh up the odds in everything I do.' Instead, I said nothing. He had to make up his own mind.

The tension built as Shawn walked back and forth on the terrace, not seeing the idyllic view, locked in an inner battle as he tried to decide. It was tempting to gamble. It would make him look cool. Also, the unknown prize might be amazing. Still, I said nothing; I knew what I would have done – but what would *he* do? At last, he said he couldn't risk losing that much money on the toss of a coin. He owned a small company and could use a million dollars wisely to help his company grow. It could change his life for the better and also help the people who worked for him and believed in him.

'I'll take the cheque,' he said.

I was pleased. Taking the cheque out of my pocket and giving it to him, I said, 'If you had gone for the coin toss, I would have lost all respect for you.'

He had made the right choice by not gambling on something he couldn't control. He got the million dollars *and* the mystery prize. The big prize was to be president of Virgin for three months. Virgin has 200 companies worldwide, employing some 50,000 people. Shawn would learn a lot. It was a golden opportunity and, by not risking everything on the flip of a coin, he had showed that Virgin would be in safe hands. He had earned the job.

I am always looking for that certain something in people like Shawn that makes them different from others. Everyone who works at Virgin is special. They aren't sheep. They think for themselves. They have good ideas that I listen to. What is the point of hiring bright people if you don't use their talent?

One of the things I try to do at Virgin is make people think about themselves and see themselves more positively. Some people call this 'reinventing yourself' – but I think we all have inbuilt strengths that need to be discovered and brought out, not reinvented. I firmly believe that anything is possible. I tell them, 'Believe in yourself. You can do it.'

And I also say, 'Be bold but don't gamble.'

I get sent thousands of proposals every week – they are people's goals and dreams. Many are unique and original with great potential, but there are too many for me to look at. Instead, my staff reads them first and weeds them out. I look at the best ones.

One plan I was offered ended in disaster. I was young and my urge to try anything almost killed me. Sadly, it killed the inventor.

A man called Richard Ellis sent me a photograph of his 'flying machine', showing it soaring over the treetops. A forerunner of the microlight, it had a three-wheeled bike beneath two large wings and it was powered by a small outboard engine. There were rotors above the pilot's head, which caused lift-off. It looked like a cross between a pterodactyl and a drawing by Leonardo da Vinci. I was curious and I invited him to show me how it worked.

When he came, we went to the local airfield with Joan and some friends. He unloaded his machine at the start of a landing strip and said you had to pedal like mad to get speed up. Then the engine would cut in and start the rotors. He said I would be the second person to try it – he was the first – but he didn't want me to fly until I had practised a bit.

'You need to get used to it first,' he explained. 'Just pedal, get some speed up, then stop.'

It looked like fun, and the photograph certainly showed that it worked, but as he advised, I was not going to rush. I sat on the machine and he gave me a cable with a rubber switch at the end, explaining that I had to bite on the switch to make the engine cut out. He assured me that as soon as the engine stopped, I would also come to a stop at the end of the runway before I got lift and became airborne.

I went through it with him. 'I bite the switch and the engine will stop?'

'Yes, exactly that.' He stepped back out of the way of the rotors and shouted, 'OK! Go!'

I put the rubber switch in my mouth and set off down the runway, pedalling like hell. The engine kicked in and I gained speed. When it seemed fast enough, I bit into the switch to stop. Nothing happened. I went even faster. I bit harder. Nothing. I reached thirty miles an hour and I could see Joan looking at me at the end of the runway as I got closer. Suddenly the flying machine took off, with me hanging on. I was flying.

I soared over some trees and kept rising even higher. At about one hundred feet I knew I had to stop it somehow. Panicking, I tugged randomly at wires and pulled them out, burning my hands on the hot engine. The engine cut out and I spun down to the ground. This was it – the moment when I would surely die, right in front of Joan. At the very last moment, a small wind flipped the machine over. A wing took the impact and I tumbled out onto the grass, safe but shocked.

A week later, Ellis took off in the flying machine. It crashed to earth and he died on impact.

His death was very sad, but people with vision do die. Mountaineers fall and test pilots crash. As a child, I knew the war hero Douglas Bader, who was a friend of my Aunt Clare's. He lost his legs in a flying accident just before the war, but he learned to walk and flew again, despite existing RAF regulations to the contrary. He was determined that he would fly and refused to give in – and neither did he moan about the blow fate had dealt him. Through him, I'd learned at a young age that you can take care but you can't protect yourself all the time – and I am sure that luck plays a very large part. Some people fly, others crash in almost exactly the same situations, but that shouldn't stop us trying. It's easy to give up when things are hard but we have to keep chasing dreams and our goals, as these exciting people did, and once we decide to do something, we should never look back, never regret it.

* * *

One decision I didn't regret was a proposal from a young American lawyer sent to me in 1984. He wanted me to invest in a new trans-Atlantic airline. Even before I read his plan I wanted to do it. Freddie Laker, a childhood hero of mine, had run Skytrain, a cut-price airline between England and America. He was a big man with bold ideas, David to the Goliath of the big airlines. He wanted to make air travel cheap enough so that more people could afford it, and it should have worked; but through no fault of his, Skytrain had collapsed in 1982. As I read this new proposal, I thought of Freddie, and the plane I'd chartered to get to Puerto Rico. It would cost a great deal of money and I told myself, 'Don't get tempted. Don't even think about it.'

But I was tempted. The idea grabbed me as I remembered the embryonic 'Virgin Airways' Caribbean jaunt. It was exciting and I could visualise it happening, and I could visualise how successful it could be.

I can make up my mind about people and ideas in sixty seconds. I rely more on gut instinct than thick reports; thus, I knew within a minute that this new airline was for me. I had travelled in other people's airlines and the experience had been ghastly. I could do it better. It was a very bold step, but worth it. Without rushing, I had to work out in my own mind what the risks were and that would involve doing some market research. I've always said that you don't need to do a lot of expensive research, or produce vast files and reports to know if something is a good idea that will work. Mostly, you need common sense and vision.

There was already a popular airline that sold cheap fares across the Atlantic, with the catchy name of People Express. I tried to call them. It seemed everyone must have wanted to fly, as their lines were busy. I tried all day but couldn't get through. They were either very busy or very inefficient. More than anything else, it was the single triggering factor that made me decide we could run an airline better than that. I spent a weekend mulling it over. By Sunday evening I had made up my mind. I would *just do it*.

On Monday morning, I called international directory enquiries and asked for the number of Boeing, the biggest American company that made planes, who were based in Seattle. Because of the time difference, I had to wait impatiently until the afternoon before I could talk to anyone, though it took several hours to get through to someone who was prepared to listen and could help me with the information I wanted, which, in simple terms, was how much was a jumbo jet? They were surprised, but they listened to me. Yes, they had a second-hand Jumbo I could have. I asked if it didn't work out, would they take it back. They agreed that they would, and that protected the downside. By the end of the call, we had worked out a good price. I felt I had done enough research and the following day I met my partners in Virgin Music to discuss it.

They said I was crazy. I said that I had worked it out carefully, weighed the pros and cons and we could afford it. If we were to grow as a company we had to have vision and aspire to reach the stars. I don't know if that was a good analogy, but it was how I felt. 'I don't want us to sit on our money like misers. It's there to be used,' I said.

They still didn't look happy, so I pressed on with my argument. I said that Virgin Music was making a lot of money, from bands like Culture Club – and the money to start an airline was less than a third of a year's profits. It was a lot, but it wasn't more than we could afford to lose. In total, it would be about two million pounds and if we kept the companies separate, Virgin Music would be protected. I pointed out that even if we lost the two million pounds, we would survive. 'It's not too big a risk. And it'll be fun.'

They winced. They weren't happy with the word 'fun'. To them, business was serious. It is, but it doesn't have to be miserable or dull. To me, having fun is important, even within a business context. In fact, it's a prime criterion in any project I undertake. I want to live life to the full. I want new goals to reach for. I argued my case with a mixture of fervour, belief in it, and business sense. They said if I really wanted an airline, why didn't I just invest in an established one? I replied that was too risky. My way would commit us to just one plane, a financial ceiling, and a business that would be set up the way we wanted to do things from the ground floor up. Established businesses were often hidebound, unable to change and adapt – and so far, we had always started up with our own ideas. It was what made Virgin and the Virgin ethos so fresh and adaptable. Starting something completely new reflected the way I wanted to live life, by setting myself huge, apparently unachievable, challenges and trying to rise above them.

I felt I had to face this challenge and make it work against all odds. In the end, my partners reluctantly agreed, but they weren't happy. I decided to use our existing name and called the airline Virgin Atlantic.

My next step was to ask Sir Freddie Laker to lunch on my houseboat home and office, where so many of my ideas have been developed, to talk about my new project. With his years of experience behind him, I knew he would be a great help and could offer sound advice. Importantly, he knew the problems in starting a new airline. Although he had gone under, it wasn't for lack of knowledge or bad business practices on his part, but because of devious and unfair methods on the part of his rivals. His airline, Skytrain, had done well until the big airlines undercut him. They had the capital to keep going and could afford to make losses. Because Freddie operated on a shoestring, he ran out of money and went bust. He sued the opposition and won millions of pounds, but by then, it was too late for him and his staff. Over lunch, he told me how an airline worked and in particular what I should look out for.

Freddie said, 'Look out for dirty tricks from British Airways. Their dirty tricks ruined me. Don't let them ruin you. Complain as loudly as possible. My mistake was that I didn't complain.'

I don't like to complain and have never cried over spilt milk. I just get on with things, but I made a mental note. 'Watch out for dirty tricks. Complain loudly.'

We discussed business class versus Freddie's tourist class and he advised me, 'Don't make it only a cheap no-frills service. The big airlines can undercut you, like they did to me. Instead, offer much better options and a good service. People want comfort and they appreciate being looked after well. And don't forget the fun. People like to have fun.'

I was pleased that I'd had this meeting with Freddie – he was a man after my own heart. When I walked him off the boat after lunch, he shook my hand and said, 'Good luck, Richard. Be ready for a great deal of stress.'

All of his advice was helpful when I had to talk to officials. Safety was a big concern with them, as was ensuring that the airline was properly funded. A properly funded airline didn't cut corners, it met all the safety regulations and criteria, it was properly insured and the passengers' money was safe when they bought tickets. Some airlines had gone under, owing a fortune to passengers. The officials' concerns and the safety regulations were important and I assured them that they would be met. Tenacity of purpose was vital when I came to dealing with contracts and negotiations and one way or another, I'd already had plenty of experience dealing with tough negotiators. Boeing was so tough over the terms of their agreements that at the end when I got the deal I wanted, they even said, 'It's easier to sell a fleet of jumbos to an American airline than just one to Virgin.'

Once I had the plane, on terms I could afford, I worked out a cash flow survival plan. Then I hired the right people and built a good team. It was hard work, but I persevered, always looking for another way around a problem. And believe me, there were endless problems. Sure enough, as Sir Freddie had predicted, BA did try dirty tricks against us. They even tried to destroy us by ruining my name. Sir Freddie said, 'Sue the bastards!' I took BA to court for libel – and won.

When Virgin Atlantic launched in 1984 not one person thought it would survive for more than a year. While we got some great press, there were also detractors. A few thought that it was impossible for a record label boss to run an airline, but they didn't appreciate the amount of effort we put into making sure we got it right. We really struggled against all odds to get going by the start of the summer holiday season, so we would have a cushion against the lean winter months when fewer people flew. By planning well we succeeded against all odds. The bosses of the big American companies said I'd fail. Now they are all out of business and I'm still there, with more airlines than ever, and growing. And when I'd said I wanted to reach for the stars, even I didn't dream that one day quite literally I would be heading for space – in Virgin Galactic.

I was bold, yes – but not foolish. I took a risk by starting up an airline. But the odds were good. They were not all or nothing, like they could have been with the winner of *The Rebel Billionaire*, and I had thought through how to manage the risks. Shawn Nelson could have won it all or lost it all on the spin of a coin. It took courage to refuse.

My next big venture was starting Virgin Trains in 1991. I got the idea when I was in Tokyo to be awarded an honorary doctorate at a university. While I was in Japan I took the opportunity to look for a site in Kyoto to build a new music Megastore. When we took the 'Shinkansen' from Tokyo to Kyoto – otherwise known as the 'Bullet Train' – I thought it was great; an amazing piece of futuristic design, smooth, fast and clean, like being on a plane.

'Why can't trains be like this in the UK?' I thought, jotting down some notes to remind me. It was fate. The following week the UK government said they would break up the old train system, British Rail, and let new businesses compete to run trains. I jumped in and said I was interested. I didn't realise how quickly the news would hit the news-papers. Headlines said: 'VIRGIN TO GO INTO TRAINS'. They said it was a bold move, though again, as with the airline, some people said I would fail. It took five years but we did it. We produced the world's most advanced tilting train – the Pendolino. It was a proud moment when my wife Joan named it *Virgin Lady*. Once again, we were ahead of everyone and I felt very proud when the TV news said we'd delivered on our promise.

From childhood, I had been taught by my parents that promises are important and should always be kept. If you can't keep a promise, they said, don't make one. Thanks to that early grounding, one thing I always try to do is to keep my word. I set my goals and stick to them. And I firmly believe that success is more than luck. You have to believe in yourself and make it happen – that way, others also believe in you.

Sometimes, I get business offers that I turn down; and while there's little point in regretting what you never had, a few opportunities have slipped away. I had the chance to invest in Ryanair, a good, no frills airline, but turned it down. Ryanair is still going strong. I turned down the chance to invest in Trivial Pursuit and a wind up radio. All of them were good ideas. But on the other side of the coin, I also turned down the chance to be a Lloyd's name. Lloyd's is the biggest insurance company in the world and insures against huge losses like hurricanes and earthquakes. In the good years when there are few natural disasters and no major claims – such as the asbestos scandal – Lloyd's names can make large profits. But in recent years, there have been some heavy runs against them with compensation to tobacco and asbestos victims. Turning down Lloyd's was a good decision. I could have lost a fortune.

Some you win and some you lose. Be glad when you win. Don't have regrets when you lose. Never look back. I know that you can't change the past, but I try to learn from it. We can't all run big airlines or trains. Many of us have more modest goals. *But whatever your dream is, go for it.* Always be aware if the risks are too random or too hard to predict – like gambling on unknown factors, or risking all on the spin of a coin – but remember, if you opt for a safe life, you will never know what it's like to win.

4. CHALLENGE YOURSELF

Aim high
Try new things
Always try
Challenge yourself

Everyone needs something to aim for. You can call it a challenge, or you can call it a goal. It is what makes us human. It was challenges that took us from being cavemen to reaching for the stars.

If you challenge yourself, you will grow, your life will change, your outlook will be positive. It's not always easy to reach your goals but that's no reason to stop. Instead, say to yourself, 'I can do it. I'll keep on trying until I win.'

For me, there are two types of challenge. One is to do the best I can at work and home. The other is to seek adventure. I try to do both. I try to stretch myself to the limit. I am driven and I love the challenge of looking for new things and new ideas.

My first big challenge came when I was four or five years old and our family went to Devon for two weeks one summer, along with two aunts and an uncle. When we got there, I ran onto the beach and stared at the sea. I longed to swim, but I had never learned how to. Auntie Joyce, who was one of dad's sisters, came and stood beside me as I gazed wistfully at the waves, and she offered me ten shillings if I learned to swim by the end of the holiday. She was very wise, knowing how instantly I respond to a challenge. I took the bet, sure I would win. Most days, the sea was rough and the waves were high, but I tried for hours to swim. Day after day, I splashed along, with one foot on the bottom, growing blue with cold, but determined to succeed and ignoring the vast quantities of seawater I swallowed – it felt like gallons. But I still couldn't swim.

'Never mind, Ricky,' Auntie Joyce said, kindly. 'There's always next year.'

I was downcast because I had lost the challenge and I was sure she would forget it next year. As we set off home in the car, I gazed out of the window. How I wished I had learned to swim. I hated losing. It was a hot day and in the 1950s the roads were very narrow, so we weren't going very fast when I saw a river. We hadn't got home so we were still really on holiday and I knew it was my last chance to win.

'Stop the car!' I shouted. My parents knew about the bet and although obviously they would not have done what I said when I was that age, I think my father knew what I wanted and how much it meant to me. He drove off the road and parked. 'What's up?' he asked, turning to me.

'Ricky wants to have another go at winning that ten shillings,' Mum said.

I jumped out of the car and stripped quickly, then ran across a field to the river. When I got to the bank, I felt scared. The river looked deep and fast, running over rocks. There was a sloping, muddy part where cows drank from and I decided that it would be easy to reach the water from there. I turned my head and saw everyone standing, watching me.

Mum smiled and waved me on. 'You can do it, Ricky!' she called.

With their massed encouragement to my rear, and Auntie Joyce's challenge driving me, I knew it was now or never. I walked through the mud and waded into the water. As soon as I got in the middle, the current caught at me and I went under and choked. I came up, and was swept downstream. Somehow, I managed to take a deep breath and relaxed, and almost floated. With a sudden sense of conviction, I knew I could do it. I put one foot on a rock and pushed off. Soon, I was swimming, splashing about awkwardly in a circle – but I'd won the bet. Through the sound of the flowing water and my splashing, I heard my family cheering on the bank. When I crawled out, I was done in, but very proud. I crawled through mud and stinging nettles to reach Auntie Joyce. Smiling widely, she held up the ten shillings.

'Well done, Ricky!' she said.

'I knew you could do it,' Mum said, offering me a dry towel. I knew I could do it too, and I was not going to give up until I had proved it.

One thing I couldn't do very well was read. I always found lessons hard at school because I was mildly dyslexic. I hated to admit defeat, but however hard I struggled, reading and writing were hard for me.

Almost perversely, this made me want to be a journalist, a job where reading and writing are always needed. When I found that my school had an essay contest, I entered. I don't know who was the most surprised when I won. I was the boy who was often caned for failing exams. But I had won an essay contest fair and square against some of the cleverest boys at school. I was thrilled and couldn't wait to tell Mum. Instead of expressing her amazement, she said quite simply, 'I knew you could win, Ricky.' Mum is one of those people who never says, 'can't'. She believes anything is possible if you try.

That success encouraged me enormously and although I was never a high achiever academically, from then on my schoolwork improved. I learned to focus on hard words and my spelling got better. I think this shows that you can achieve almost anything – but you have to make the effort. I didn't stop challenging myself. I went on from winning that essay prize to starting *Student* magazine. I think I wanted to prove that the boy who was caned for not being able to read or write well could do it.

As I grew older, out in the wider world I faced bigger challenges. I seemed to run on high energy and craved adventure. Danger tempted me. I had already set a record for being the first to cross the Atlantic in a balloon with Per. In the New Year of 1990 Per and I decided to cross the Pacific Ocean, from Japan to the USA. It was a far more dangerous venture, across 8,000 miles of open sea. No one had ever done it before.

I spent Christmas on a small island off Japan with my family and friends. It was very lovely and peaceful there, with that kind of soft, timeless, misty look you get in Japanese paintings. There was a river, flowing past rocks and groves of willows and bamboo, where I watched fishermen catching fish with tame cormorants. Their lives seemed calm and tranquil and I wondered if they were happy, or did they have the same dreams and fears of us all? With their ancient traditions and way of life, perhaps they had come to terms with time in a way I never had. What would they think of my constant rushing about? I only knew that challenges were what drove me onwards.

Because Joan doesn't like to see me leave on the more dangerous challenges, and the children had to go back to school, I had just waved them off at Tokyo to return to London, and was walking with my parents along the concourse to catch an internal flight to where our balloon was waiting, when on big news-screens I saw rescue helicopters winching up a body from the sea. I knew instinctively that it was our Japanese rival, Fumio Niwa. He had taken off into high winds early that morning, to beat us to it, but his balloon had torn and he ditched into the freezing sea. It was so stormy, he couldn't be rescued in time, and he died from exposure. Watching the final scene unfold on television was doubly shocking for me, because only recently, I had been laughing and joking with him.

After that tragedy, understandably, I was shaken. But I had promised to go and everything was ready for the attempt. I felt that I couldn't withdraw, so resigned myself to fate. Whatever the danger, I wouldn't give in, and I think Joan understood.

Our plan with the balloon was to cross the ocean on one of the jet streams that girdle the earth from

30,000 to 35,000 feet up. They travel as fast as a river in full flood. Below that, the winds are slower. Our problem was the height of our giant balloon. It was over 300 feet from the top to the bottom of the capsule. When we broke through into the jet stream, the top half of the balloon and the bottom would travel at different speeds. Anything could happen.

We put on our parachutes and clipped ourselves to the life rafts so that if anything went wrong we would not waste valuable time doing that later. Then we fired the burners. As we rose, the top of the balloon hit the bottom of the jet stream. It was like hitting a glass ceiling. We burned more fuel, but the winds were so strong they kept pushing us down. We burned even more fuel – and at last broke through. The top of the balloon was caught by the fast current and took off like a rocket. It was flying along at a crazy angle at 115 miles an hour. The capsule was still going at 25 mph. It felt like a thousand horses were dragging us apart. We were too high to jump out and feared the balloon would be torn in two, and the heavy capsule would hurtle thousands of feet down to the sea.

But, at the last moment, the capsule shot through the glass ceiling and the balloon righted itself.

The ferocity and power of the jet stream and the fact that we had done it and survived awed me. There was a kind of wild and terrifying exhilaration to the experience of being alone in all that space. It seemed such a fragile reality that all that kept us up there was – literally – hot air.

We flew along at great speed, faster than we thought possible. (In the air, speed, as on water, is usually given in knots. I have given mph in order for it to be clearer.) Seven hours later it was time to lose the first empty fuel tank. For some reason, it seemed safer to drop down out of the jet stream to do this, although everything we did was new and experimental. We cut off the burners and went down into a slower zone. At once, the capsule acted like a brake, but the balloon still hurtled along. Through the video camera on the bottom of the capsule, we could clearly see the angry grey sea 25,000 feet below us, with white caps and dark troughs. I wondered if we would end up in it.

Per pressed the button to release the empty fuel tank and sickeningly, we lurched sideways. I fell against Per as everything slid towards us. To our horror we found that two full tanks – weighing a ton apiece – as well as the empty one had fallen off one side. Not only were we lopsided and off balance, but we didn't have enough fuel to control our height and find the right wind pattern, and it seemed highly unlikely that we could possibly reach the USA. Three tons lighter, the balloon soared upwards. We hit the jet stream so fast we shot through the glass ceiling like a bullet and kept on rising. Per let some air out of the balloon, but still we soared up and up.

We had been warned that at 43,000 feet the glass dome of our capsule would explode and our lungs and eyeballs would be sucked out of our bodies. At 41,000 feet we entered the unknown. Mesmerised, we watched the altimeter, like birds watching a snake, as it wound up to a frightening 42,500 feet. We had no idea what might happen. We were not only higher than any balloon had ever been, but higher than most aircraft had ever flown. At last, the balloon cooled and we started to fall fast. Again, we watched the altimeter, this time in reverse, as we hurtled downwards. We didn't want to burn extra fuel, but we had to, to stop falling. We couldn't come down in the sea because there was no one in the vast space of the Pacific to rescue us.

We would have to last for another thirty hours on little fuel; and in order to reach land we had to fly faster than any balloon had ever flown before. That meant staying right in the centre of the jet stream, a space just one hundred yards wide – the exact height of the balloon. It seemed impossible.

The final straw was when we lost radio contact. We had been going for hours and Per was worn out. He lay down and fell into an instant, deep sleep. I was on my own. I don't believe in God, but that day it felt as if a guardian angel had entered the capsule and was helping us along. From the dials I saw that we had started to speed up, faster and faster. I thought I was dreaming and slapped my face to make sure I was awake. We went from 80 mph, through 180, then 200, then 240. This was unheard of. It seemed like a miracle.

I was so exhausted I felt spacey, but with Per asleep I had to stay on watch. When I saw strange, flickering lights in the glass dome, I thought they were spirits. I watched them as if in a dream, until I realised that burning lumps of gas were falling all around. It was minus 70 degrees outside. If a fireball hit the frozen glass dome, it would explode.

'Per!' I yelled. 'Wake up! We're on fire!'

Per woke up fast. He knew at once what to do. 'Take her up to 40,000 feet where there's no oxygen,' he said. 'Then the fire will go out.'

We rose, with the burning gas still scattering around us, passing our previous maximum of 42,500

feet and rising. At just under 43,000 feet, I anticipated the capsule exploding and imagined my eyeballs and lungs being sucked out in red blobs of jelly,
like a horror movie. To my great relief, the flames
died and we started down again. But we had wasted
precious fuel. Then the radio suddenly crackled into
life. A voice said, 'War's broken out in the Gulf. The
Americans are bombing Baghdad.' It seemed strange
and almost irrelevant that we were alone almost on
the edge of space and a war had just started on earth.

On the radio, our ground crew told us that the jet
stream we were riding had turned and we'd loop
back to Japan. We had to get into a lower jet stream
at once, one that would take us to the Arctic, but this
stream was far slower. In order to reach land, our
average speed couldn't drop under 170 mph – which
was twice as fast as any balloonist had ever flown.
We dropped down to 18,000 feet and hit the slow
northern jet stream. Just when it looked as if we
would have to start planning a drop into the sea, the
ground crew told us we had joined another jet
stream heading in the right direction. In a narrow
band 30,000 feet up, we flew hour after hour at a
miraculous 200 plus mph in a lop-sided capsule. We
finally landed in a blizzard, on a frozen lake in the
far north of Canada in a wild area two hundred
times the size of Britain.

We wrenched open the hatch and clambered
outside. We hugged each other and danced a little jig
in the snow. The silver balloon envelope had draped
itself across the pine trees and was being shredded by
the wind. Then we realised two things: the capsule
wasn't going to blow up, and it was minus 60
degrees outside. Unless we got back inside, we'd get

frostbite. We crawled inside the capsule and I made radio contact with Watson Lake Flight Service.

'We've done it. We've arrived. We're all in one piece.'

'Where are you?'

'We've landed on a lake surrounded by trees.'

'It's a frozen lake,' came the laconic Canadian voice. 'It's quite safe. The only trouble is that there are about 800,000 lakes in your vicinity and they've all got plenty of trees.'

We had to wait in our capsule for another eight hours. Per had frostbite in one of his feet, and I had frostbite in a finger. We huddled together, half-asleep, eating our supplies, desperate for warmth as the snow and wind howled around our metal capsule. We had landed over 300 miles from the nearest habitation, 150 miles from the nearest road.

At last we heard the thudding sound of a helicopter's blades. It got louder and louder, and then the helicopter circled overhead and landed beside us.

It was another four hours' flight to Yellowknife. When we landed at a tiny airfield, the yellow fluorescent lights made blurred circles in the driving snow. We crunched across the snow to the hangar. Gusts of flakes blew across us as we opened the door and stepped inside.

There was Will Whitehorn, Virgin Group's Corporate and Brand Development Director, Mum, Dad, Per's wife Helen, and some people from Yellowknife. I almost didn't recognise anyone since they were all wearing strange bulky clothing: bright-red padded jackets and thermal trousers. They roared with delight when we came in.

'Have a cold beer!' Will shouted. 'It's all there is!'

Per and I ripped off the ringpulls and sprayed everyone there.

'You've made it!' said Mum.

'Never again!' said Dad.

'What do you mean?' Per joked. 'We're going round the world next time. If those fuel tanks had stayed on we'd be over England now!'

I laughed, but I knew I couldn't turn down a challenge. We made the attempt a couple of years later.

Just before we had left to cross the Pacific, my daughter, Holly, sent me a fax from London. She wrote, 'I hope you don't land in the water and have a bad landing. I hope you have a good landing and land on dry land.'

It seemed a perfect metaphor for my life. I have been lucky. So far, I have nearly always landed on dry land. I think the writer and mountain climber James Ullman summed it all up when he said something like, 'Challenge is the core and mainspring of all human action. If there's an ocean, we cross it. If there's a disease we cure it. If there's a wrong, we right it. If there's a record, we break it. And if there's a mountain, we climb it.'

I totally agree and believe we should all continue to challenge ourselves.

5. STAND ON YOUR OWN FEET

Rely on yourself
Chase your dreams but live in the real world
Work together

'If you want milk, don't sit on a stool in the middle of a field in the hope that the cow will back up to you.' This old saying could have been one of my mother's quotes. She would have added, 'Go on, Ricky. Don't just sit around. Catch the cow.'

An old recipe for rabbit pie reputedly said, 'First catch the rabbit.' Note, that it didn't say, 'First buy the rabbit,' or, 'Sit on your bottom until someone gives you a rabbit.'

Lessons like this, taught by Mum from when I was a toddler, are what have made me stand on my own feet. I was trained to think for myself and get things done. It's what the British as a nation used to believe in, but there are some kids today who seem to want everything handed to them on a plate. I'd been lucky enough to have good parents.

My first lesson in self-sufficiency was when I was about four years old. We'd been out somewhere and on the way back Mum stopped the car a few miles from our house and told me to find my own way home across the fields. She made it a game, one I was happy to play. It was an early challenge I've never forgotten. As I grew older, these lessons grew harder. Early one winter morning, when I was about twelve and home for half term from boarding school, Mum shook me awake and told me to get dressed. It was dark and cold, but I crawled out of bed. After breakfast in the kitchen – probably hot and nourishing porridge, to sustain me – I was given a packed lunch and an apple. 'I'm sure you will find some water along the way,' Mum said, as she waved me off on a fifty-mile bicycle ride to the south coast. It was still dark when I set off on my own with a map in case I got lost. I spent the night with a relative and returned home the next day. When I walked into the warm kitchen where Mum and Lindi were, I felt very proud, sure I would be greeted by cheers. Instead, Mum said, 'Well done, Ricky. Was that fun? Now run along, the vicar wants you to chop some logs for him.'

To some people this might sound harsh. But the members of my family love and care for each other very much. We are a close-knit unit, totally loyal. Those early lessons, which increased as we grew, were because my parents wanted us to be strong and to rely on ourselves, to be free, independent spirits. Remember, they and their generation had been through two world wars and mollycoddling was not in their vocabulary. Dad was always there for us, but Mum was the one who drove us to want to do our best. I learned about business and money from her. She would say things like, 'The winner takes all,' and, 'Chase your dreams'. Mum knew that losing wasn't fair, but it is life. It's not a good idea to teach children that they can win all the time. In the real world, people struggle and there are winners and losers and sometimes injustices that we have to rise above.

When I was born, Dad was just starting out in law and money was tight. Mum didn't moan. She had two aims. One was to find useful tasks for my sisters and me because being idle was frowned on. The other was to find ways to make money to help the family budget. At home, my parents didn't have any secrets from us; they told us what was going on and we talked business at dinner. I know some parents keep their work away from the kids and won't share their problems, but I believe their children never really learn the value of money, or about income and bills. Sometimes, when they get into the real world they can't cope. We, on the other hand, knew what the real world was about because it was discussed in front of us. My sister, Lindi, and I helped Mum with her various moneymaking projects. It was fun and made for a great sense of teamwork within our family.

I have tried to bring up Holly and Sam in the same way, although I have been lucky to have more money than my parents had. I still think my mum's rules were good and I believe Holly and Sam have learned the value of money.

With a family to look after, Mum couldn't go out to work – and not many mothers did in the 1950s. Instead, she looked about for something she could do at home and came up with making little wooden tissue boxes and waste paper bins. Her workshop was the garden shed and it was our job to help her. We enjoyed painting the boxes and stacking them up until there were enough to dispatch. Dad even helped in his spare time by making clamps that held the glued parts together. Mum took samples around to show to store buyers, and when Harrods ordered them, business and sales boomed. She also took in French and German students as paying guests, so her days were full of domestic chores. Hard work and fun were family traits and we all developed entrepreneurial skills, perhaps from having to make money in the lean years after the war.

Mum's sister, Aunt Clare, was batty about black Welsh sheep and got the idea of starting a company to sell mugs with black sheep on them. As the sheep gained in popularity, she launched into other ranges, getting ladies in the village to knit woollies with sheep motifs on them. The company became very successful and is still going strong. Years later, when I was running Virgin Records, Aunt Clare phoned me to say that one of her sheep had started singing. I didn't laugh. Her ideas were always clever. Instead, I followed the sheep around with a tape recorder. 'Baa Baa Black Sheep' became a hit, reaching number 4 in the charts.

I went from small cottage industries to setting up Virgin worldwide. While the basic rules were the same – cash flow, profit and loss – the risks became bigger and I learned to be bold in my dealings and ideas. Although I listen carefully to everyone, I make up my own mind and just do it. I believe in myself and in my goals and have always tried to expand my horizons without losing my ideals, or the lessons of integrity, honesty and respect for other people that I was taught at home as a child.

I lost faith in myself only once, and that was in 1986. By then, Virgin was one of Britain's largest private companies, with 4,000 members of staff. Sales had increased by 60 per cent from the year before and like many other companies that had risen so fast and visibly, I was told I should go public. I wasn't sure and certainly two of my partners were not keen, because they knew me well. They said I would hate losing control. But what really prompted my decision was that I felt we had been badly let down by our bankers. Like many companies who dealt around the world, a great deal of our money was slow to come in, and when it did, it arrived in big lump payments. So, although we were liquid on paper and had substantial profits, we worked on a revolving overdraft facility.

At the time the crunch happened, we had a £3 million overdraft, and were expecting a cheque to the tune of £6 million any day from the US. On top of that, we were looking forward to profits of £20 million at the end of the financial year. There was no doubt that overall we were in a healthy fiscal position – but our bank didn't think we were. The sole reason for their disapproval seemed to be because I had started Virgin Atlantic and it was only recently that Skytrain had gone bust in a very public way. At any rate, my manager came to see me with the bad news: they were pulling the plug. I'm afraid I was so angry that I literally pushed him out of my house, one of the few times when I have lost my temper like that. Then I had to phone around the world, pulling in some of our money fast and doing some short-term borrowing.

However, we were still in choppy water and my best option seemed to be to go public. By 1986 everyone was heading for the City. Everyone who had bought shares in British Telecom had doubled their money.

I will never forget going into the City to see the lines of people queuing up to buy Virgin shares. We had already had over 70,000 postal applicants to buy Virgin shares, but these people had left it until the last day, 13 November 1986. I walked up and down the queue thanking people for their confidence, and a number of their replies stuck in my mind:

'We're not going on holiday this year; we're putting our savings into Virgin.'

'Go on, Richard, prove us right.'

'We're banking on you, Richard.'

At one point I noticed that the press photographers were taking pictures of my feet. I couldn't understand it. Then I looked down and noticed with a shock that, in the rush to get dressed, I had put on shoes that didn't match.

The flotation of Virgin attracted more applications from the public than any other stock-market debut issue, apart from the massive government privatisations. Over 100,000 private individuals applied for our shares, and the Post Office drafted in twenty extra staff to cope with the mail sacks.

It wasn't long, though, before I came to hate the ways of the City. They weren't for me. Instead of a casual meeting with my partners on my houseboat to discuss what bands to sign, I had to ask a board of directors. Many of them had no idea at all what the music business was all about. They didn't see how a hit record could make millions overnight. Instead of being able to sign someone who was hot, before our rivals did, I had to wait four weeks for a board meeting – and by then, it was too late. Or they'd say things like, 'Sign the Rolling Stones? My wife doesn't like them. Janet Jackson? Who's she?'

I have always made fast decisions and acted on my instinct but I felt stifled by red tape, boardroom committees and doing it by the book. I hated having to sit at the top of a long polished table, surrounded by pinstriped suits, while I tried to explain what Virgin was about – when I didn't even have an office and my 'desk' was a comfortable armchair on my houseboat and a yellow legal pad to make notes in. Most of all, I no longer felt that I was standing on my own feet. We doubled our profits but Virgin shares started to slip and, for the first time in my life, I was depressed.

Then there was a huge stock market crash and shares dropped fast. It wasn't my fault, but I felt that I was letting down all the people who had bought Virgin shares. Many were friends and family as well as our staff. But many were like the couple who had given me their life savings. I made up my mind. I would buy all the shares back – at the price everyone had paid for them. I didn't have to, but I didn't want to let people down. I personally raised the £182 million needed, but it was worth it to keep my freedom, reputation and character.

The day that Virgin became a private company again was like landing safely after a record attempt in a powerboat or a balloon. I felt nothing but relief.

Once again, I was the captain of my ship and master of my fate.

I believe in myself. I believe in the hands that work, in the brains that think, and in the hearts that love.

6. LIVE THE MOMENT

Love life and live it to the full
Enjoy the moment
Reflect on your life
Make every second count
Don't have regrets

I was about to set off on a round the world hot-air balloon race in 1997, once again with Per, and with Alex Ritchie, the brilliant engineer who had designed the capsule that would take us 24,000 miles. Before we left that morning, in the quiet of my hotel room in Marrakech, I woke early and wrote a long letter to my children, in case I didn't return. I started the letter by saying,

Dear Holly and Sam,
Life can seem rather unreal at times. Alive and well and loving one day. No longer there the next. As you both know I always had the urge to live life to its full . . .

I folded the letter into a small square and put it in my pocket.

We had done all the checks, and were ready to go. Ten, nine, eight, seven, six, five ... Per counted down and I concentrated on working the cameras. My hand kept darting down to check my parachute buckle. I tried not to think about the huge balloon above us, and the six vast fuel tanks strapped round our capsule. Four, three, two, one ... and Per threw the lever which fired the bolts which severed the anchor cables and we lifted silently and swiftly into the sky. There was no roar of the burners: our ascent was like that of a child's party balloon. We just rose up, up and away and then, as we caught the morning breeze, we headed over Marrakech.

The emergency door was still open as we soared up, and we waved down at the, by now, little people. Every detail of Marrakech, its square pink walls, the large town square, the green courtyards and fountains hidden behind high walls, was laid out below us. By 10,000 feet it became cold and the air grew thin. We shut the trap door. From now on we were on our own. We were pressurised, and the pressure would mount.

We flew serenely for the rest of the day. The views over the Atlas Mountains were exhilarating, their jagged peaks capped with snow gleaming up at us in the glorious sunshine.

As we approached the Algerian border we had a shock when the Algerians informed us that we were heading straight for Béchar, their top military base. They told us that we could not fly over it: 'You are not, repeat not, authorised to enter this area,' said the fax.

We had no choice.

I spent about two hours on the satellite phone to Mike Kendrick, our flight controller, and tried various British ministers. Eventually André Azoulay, the Moroccan minister who had helped us with the launch in Morocco, came to the rescue again. He explained to the Algerians that we could not change our direction and that we did not have powerful cameras on board. They accepted this, and relented.

By 5 p.m. we were flying at 30,000 feet. Per started firing the burners to heat the air inside the envelope. Although we burnt for an hour, just after 6 p.m. the balloon started losing height steadily.

'Something's wrong with the theory here,' Per said.

'What's the matter?' I asked.

'I don't know.'

Per was firing the burners continuously, but the balloon was still heading down. We lost 1,000 feet, and then another 500 feet. It was getting colder all the time as the sun disappeared. It was clear that the helium was rapidly contracting, becoming a dead weight on top of us.

'We've got to dump ballast,' Per said. He was frightened. We all were.

We pulled levers to dump the lead weights which were on the bottom of the capsule. These were meant to be held in reserve for about two weeks. They fell away from the capsule and I saw them on my video screen dropping like bombs. I had a horrible feeling that this was just the start of a disaster.

It was now getting dark. Without the lead weights, we steadied for a while, but then the balloon started falling once more. This time the fall was faster. We dropped 2,000 feet in one minute; 2,000 feet the next. My ears went numb and then popped, and I felt my stomach rising up, pressing against my ribcage. We were at only 15,000 feet. I tried to stay calm, focusing intently on the cameras and the altimeter, rapidly going through the options available. We needed to jettison the fuel tanks. But, as soon as we did so, the trip was over. I bit my lip. We were somewhere over the Atlas Mountains in darkness, and we were heading for a horrible crash-landing. None of us spoke. I made some rapid calculations.

'At this rate of fall we've got seven minutes,' I said.

'OK,' Per said. 'Open the hatch. Depressurise.'

We opened the trap door at 12,000 feet, dropping to 11,000 feet, and with a breathtaking rush of freezing air the capsule depressurised. Alex and I started throwing everything overboard: food, water, oil cans, anything that wasn't built into the capsule. Everything. Even a wodge of dollars. For five minutes, this stalled our fall. There was no question of continuing. We just had to save our lives.

'It's not enough,' I said, seeing the altimeter drop to 9,000 feet. 'We're still falling.'

'OK, I'm going out on the roof,' Alex said. 'The fuel tanks have got to go.'

Since Alex practically built the capsule, he knew exactly how to undo the locks. The burners roared overhead, casting a fierce orange light over us.

'Have you parachuted before?' I shouted at Alex.

'Never,' he said.

'That's your ripcord,' I said, pushing his hand to it.

'It's 7,000 feet and falling,' Per called out. '6,600 feet now.'

Alex climbed through the hatch, on to the top of the capsule. It was difficult to feel how fast we were dropping. My ears had now blocked. If the locks were frozen and Alex wasn't able to free the fuel cans, we'd have to jump. We had only a few minutes left. I looked up at the hatch and rehearsed what we would have to do: one hand to the rim, step out, and jump into the darkness. My hand instinctively felt for my parachute. I checked to see that Per was wearing his. Per was watching the altimeter. The numbers were falling fast.

We had only 6,000 feet to play with and it was dark – no, 5,500 feet. If Alex was up there for another minute, we'd have 3,500 feet. I stood with my head through the hatch, paying out the strap and watching Alex as he worked his way round the top of the capsule. It was pitch-dark below us and freezing cold. We couldn't see the ground. The phone and fax were ringing incessantly. Ground control must have been wondering what the hell we were doing.

'One's off,' Alex shouted through the hatch.

'3,700 feet,' Per said.

'Another one,' Alex said.

'3,400 feet.'

'Another one.'

'2,900 feet, 2,400.'

It was too late to bale out. By the time we'd jumped, we'd be smashing into the mountains rushing up to meet us.

'Get back in,' Per yelled. 'Now.'

Alex fell back through the hatch.

We braced ourselves. Per threw the lever to disconnect a fuel tank. If this bolt failed, we'd be dead in about sixty seconds. The tank dropped away and the balloon jerked to an abrupt halt. It felt like an elevator hitting the ground. We were flattened into our seats, my head crammed down into my shoulders. Then the balloon began to rise. We watched the altimeter: 2,600, 2,700, 2,800 feet. We were safe. In ten minutes we were up past 3,000 feet and the balloon was heading back into the night sky.

I knelt on the floor beside Alex and hugged him.

'Thank God you're with us,' I said. 'We'd be dead without you.'

They say that a dying man reviews his life in the final seconds before his death. In my case this was not true. As we hurtled down towards becoming a fireball on the Atlas Mountains and I thought that we were going to die, all I could think of was that, if I escaped with my life, I would never do this again.

Throughout that first night, we fought to keep control of the balloon. As dawn approached, we made preparations to land. Below was the Algerian desert, an inhospitable place at the best of times, more so in a country in the middle of a civil war.

The desert was not the yellow sandy sweep of soft dunes which you expect from watching *Lawrence of Arabia*. The bare earth was red and rocky, as barren as the surface of Mars, the rocks standing upright like vast termites' nests. Alex and I sat up on the roof of the capsule, marvelling at the dawn as it broke over the desert. We were aware this was a day that we might not have survived to see. The rising sun and the growing warmth of the day seemed infinitely precious. Watching the balloon's shadow slip across the desert floor, it was hard to believe it was the same contraption that had plummeted towards the Atlas Mountains in the middle of the night.

The still-attached fuel tanks were blocking Per's view, so Alex talked him in to land. As we neared the ground Alex shouted out:

'Power line ahead!'

Per shouted back that we were in the middle of the Sahara and there couldn't possibly be a power line. 'You must be seeing a mirage,' he bawled.

Alex insisted that he come up and see for himself: we had managed to find the only power line in the Sahara.

Despite the vast barren desert all around us, within minutes of our landing there were signs of life. A group of Berber tribesmen materialised from the rocks. At first they kept their distance. We were about to offer them some water and the few remaining supplies, when we heard the clattering roar of gunship helicopters. They must have tracked us on their radar. As quickly as they had appeared, the Berber vanished. Two helicopters landed close by, throwing up clouds of dust, and soon we were surrounded by impassive soldiers holding machine guns, apparently unsure where to point them.

'Allah,' I said, encouragingly.

For a moment they stood still, but their curiosity got the better of them and they came forward. We showed their officer around the capsule, and he marvelled at the remaining fuel tanks.

As I looked at the capsule standing in the red sand, and relived the harrowing drop towards the Atlas Mountains, I renewed my vow that I would never attempt this again. In perfect contradiction to this, at the back of my mind I also knew that, as soon as I was home and had talked to the other balloonists who were trying to fly round the world, I would agree to have one last go. It's an irresistible challenge and it's now buried too deeply inside for me to give up.

My next attempt to go around the world in a hot-air balloon again started in Marrakech on 18 December 1998. This time, we sailed serenely over the Atlas Mountains and kept going until we heard on the radio that Colonel Qaddafi had thrown a spanner in the works by banning us from flying over Libya. I faxed him an impassioned letter and eventually he relented. But it was the first of many such difficulties. Time and time again over the next few days my diary describes the euphoria of sailing over Mount Ararat where Noah landed the Ark, to following the path of Alexander the Great towards Afghanistan, safely passing between Mount Everest and K2 – and then the low of being refused permission to fly over a part of China that we had been expressly forbidden to go into. Even Tony Blair was drawn into the battle to get permission, which was finally granted by the Chinese. This was just as well because, unable to control the winds, we had no option but to remain on course. After sailing over Mount Fiji at dawn, we followed the same path as our successful Pacific crossing and looked set to fly over America, along with Santa and his reindeer on Christmas Eve.

As I drifted off to sleep just before America, I thought that this is almost too much for one person in their lifetime, to have such fantastic experiences, and to be so fortunate. But the weather had beaten us to it. I woke to find we had run into an invisible wall that seemed to extend along the entire US coastline. Unable to break through, with the nearest land being Hawaii, I thought we would probably die, so I wrote my will, asking to be buried in a certain spot if my body was recovered. Some sixty miles short of Hawaii we crashed into the sea, and once again I was rescued by a helicopter.

On Boxing Day, I flew to Necker to join my family and my best friends. But nobody was in the Big House when I walked in. It seemed slightly surreal to find the place entirely deserted. I found everyone at the very far end of the island – at the very spot I had designated in my will. The previous day, when I thought I would die, I had asked to be buried in this very special place, surrounded by those whom I loved the most in the world. It was strange to be there in person with those people, looking around and thinking, My God, what a different kind of party this could have been.

The experience didn't put me off my thirst for dangerous ventures. I love balloons and have one of my own. It's a small balloon with a wicker basket, like the one in *Around the World in Eighty Days*, just the right size to take my family and friends up. The sky is one of the most peaceful places I know. Gliding silently along, apart from the rest of the world, makes me feel at one with nature. Nobody can phone you, nobody can stop you. You are free. You look down on towns and fields and people who don't know you're there. You can fly alongside a wild swan and hear the beat of its wings. You can look into the eyes of an eagle.

Balloons have taught me to reflect more. On earth, my life is fast and hectic, each moment full. It can be too busy. We all need our own space and it's good to pause and do nothing. It gives us time to think. It recharges our bodies as well as our minds. I often think of the fishermen I watched that Christmas in Japan. It's in our nature to strive – so I wondered what they looked for in life? They seemed content fishing and feeding their families. They didn't seem driven to set up fish canning empires and, as far as I knew, they didn't want to cross the Pacific in a balloon or climb Mount Everest. They took each day as it came. They lived the moment and perhaps this is what gave them peace of mind.

My grandmother, Dorothy Huntley-Flindt, lived life to the full. At the age of 89 she became the oldest person in Britain to pass the advanced Latin American ballroom-dancing exam. She was 90 when she became the oldest person to hit a hole in one at golf. She never stopped learning. In her mid-nineties she read Stephen Hawking's book, *A Brief History of Time*, which may make her one of the few people to have read it *all the way through!* Shortly before her death at the age of 99 she went on a cruise round the world. She laughed about it when she was left behind in Jamaica with only her swimming costume. Her attitude was, you've got one go in life, so you should make the most of it.

My parents are getting on and are into their eighties now. Like Granny did, they still hop on and off planes and travel around the world. They have been there at the start and end of all my adventures, cheering me on. They even went looking for me when Per and I were lost in the wilds of the frozen North after our balloon came down in a blizzard in Canada. Their example reminds me to enjoy life.

In 1999, with Mum and Dad, I bought Ulusaba, a private game reserve in South Africa, set in 10,000 acres of wilderness in the heart of the Sabi Sands Game Reserve that borders the sprawling Kruger National Park. Here, we built a lovely house and we spend time together as a family. In fact, I am so aware of how precious time with them is, I ration myself to only fifteen minutes of business a day when we're together. I rarely use modern gadgets like email or mobile phones, but in Africa I did learn to use a satellite phone to keep in touch with the office. When we're camping by a river in the Serengeti, or watching the game come down to drink in the evening, I will quietly make my calls, then join the family. The two worlds are so far apart that business is the interloper. Many bosses, who spend all day in their office, are baffled. They ask, 'How can you do it all in just fifteen minutes?'

I say, 'It's easy. *Make every second count.*' That is true in both my business and personal life.

I am able to say that now I am older and perhaps wiser, but it wasn't always the case. My first wife, Kristen, got very irate because I was always on the phone. She said I spent my life working and couldn't draw the line between work and home. She was right. Part of the trouble was, I worked from home and simply couldn't resist picking up the phone when it rang, which it did, non-stop. I wished I could just let it ring – but I never knew when it might lead to a nice deal.

Even today, even when I am relaxing, I never stop thinking. My brain is working all the time when I am awake, churning out ideas. Because Virgin is a worldwide company, I find I need to be awake much of the time, so it's fortunate that one of the things I am very good at is catnapping, catching an hour or two of sleep at a time. Of all the skills I have learned, that one is vital for me. On a bus between Hong Kong and China for example, when nothing much is happening, I will sleep. I wake refreshed and ready to go for long hours. It's also a very good way of switching off. Churchill and Maggie Thatcher were masters of the catnap and I use their example in my own life.

The Spanish painter, Dali, had a unique way to savour the moment. When he was bored with life, he would walk in his garden above the sea. He would pick a perfect peach, warm from the sun, holding it in his hand to admire its golden skin. Closing his eyes, he would sniff it, breathing in deeply as its warm perfume filled his senses. Then he would take a single bite. His mouth would fill with luscious juice. He would savour it slowly. Then he would spit out the mouthful and throw the peach into the sea below. He said it was a perfect moment and he gained more from that single, unrequited bite than from gorging on a basket of peaches.

In a way, regrets are like wanting the peach you have thrown away. It's gone, but you are filled with remorse. You wish you hadn't thrown it away. You want it back. I believe the one thing that helps you capture the moment is to have no regrets. Regrets weigh you down and hold you back in the past when you should move on.

It's hard to lose out on a business deal, but harder to suffer from guilt. We all do things we wish we hadn't. Sometimes – usually in the middle of the night when you can't sleep – they seem like big mistakes, but later, when you look back, they turn out to be small. Regrets, which lead to a sense of guilt, can give you sleepless nights. But I believe the past is the past. You can't change it. So even if sometimes you get things wrong, regrets are wasted and you should move on.

An example of this is when Kristen and I went on our honeymoon to Mexico. She deliberately chose the island of Cozumel where there were no phones and where no one could get in touch with me. At first, I found it hard being so far out of reach, but there were so many things to do that gradually I unwound. After two weeks we headed for the Yucatan Peninsula, where Mayan ruins could be explored by jeep or horseback. One night in a bar in a small port there, I started chatting to a couple of tourists, who said off Yucatan was the best place in the world for marlin and sailfish. I had never done any deep-sea fishing and instantly was smitten with the idea. I asked around and fixed it up with some fishermen to take us out in their boat the next day. We were at the harbour early, but despite it appearing to be bright and sunny, the skipper refused to go, saying it looked like there might be a storm.

I thought he was holding out for more money. We were returning home the following day and this was my only chance. Eager to go, I said I would pay him double. The others from the bar who had arranged to go with us also said they'd pay double and the skipper changed his mind. The tourists were right – the fishing was amazing. Marlin and sailfish seemed to leap out of the water to grab our baited hooks, though landing them was quite a fight. We'd had an exciting day of sport and I was in the middle of playing a marlin when I noticed that it was growing dark. Suddenly, a fisherman cut my line with a knife and the marlin vanished into the deep. I was a bit shocked. We had released our other catch, but I wasn't happy with the idea of a big fish swimming around still attached to yards of line. But getting out of the approaching storm was pressing and I didn't argue. In a rising cold wind, the crew started the engine to head home. But the rudder jammed so the boat couldn't steer and we went round in circles. The storm grew stronger, the sea grew wilder, and towering waves broke over us. It was the worst storm I had ever experienced. People were being sick, Kristen was shaking with fear and cold, and the boat was being pounded hard. I was sure she was about to break up and sink.

After an hour, the worst of the storm seemed to have passed. There was calm and the sky was filled with a strange and ominous light. In fact, we were in the eye of the storm and a greater danger was approaching. I stared at the horizon and was terrified when I saw a solid black line coming closer across the waves. It was the far wall of the storm and looked alarming. I was sure we would all die when it hit us.

Kristen, who was American and knew that kind of ocean, quickly weighed up the odds of remaining in the boat and probably going down with it, or of swimming for dry land, hoping to beat the storm. She was a strong swimmer and she said we should swim for the shore, which was two miles away. Everyone said we were mad, but we insisted and the fishermen gave us a plank of wood to hold onto and we jumped overboard. It seemed a crazy thing to do. I went from being scared of drowning, to the terror of being eaten by sharks. We were swept far down the coast but kept swimming, helped along by the huge waves which rolled in ahead of the storm.

Two hours later, half frozen, we dragged our way up through the surf and onto the beach, where we collapsed, lacking all energy. As soon as we could move again, we stumbled through stinking black mangrove swamps to the village for help. We found a big boat to go back to sea to rescue the others, but we ran into an even bigger storm and were tossed back to shore. When the storm cleared, they searched for two days, but found nothing, not a hint of wreckage, or any bodies. It was terrible. We flew home, quiet and depressed while I struggled with guilt.

I could have tried to live with the guilt. Instead, although it was tragic, I realised that I had to apply logic to it, just to be able to move on mentally and emotionally. I told myself that the fishermen took the money against their better judgement, but they didn't have to. It was the state of the boat that was the problem, and that wasn't my fault. If a ferry goes down with the loss of life, it's not the passengers who are at fault, but the captain or the owners.

The story of the lost boat came out when my autobiography, *Losing My Virginity*, was published some years later. The *Daily Mirror* sent a reporter to Mexico to find out what had happened. To my relief, they found the boat and the crew alive and well. The tide and the winds had taken them many miles down the coast, exactly as Kristen and I had been carried down the coast, but they'd gone that much further.

It took time to fix their boat and there was no radio and no phones to keep in touch. After we had left for home, they sailed safely into the harbour. I didn't know any of this and I could have spent years living with needless remorse.

One lesson I learned from that experience, and have tried to follow ever since, is to be nice to people. At the turn of the millennium, I heard a vicar talking on Radio 4. He said if everyone would befriend their enemy the world would be a more pleasant and peaceful place. So the next day, I telephoned Colin Marshall, my old antagonist at BA, and invited him to lunch. I don't think he could work out what I was up to, but he came. I invited him to be the chairman of my Lottery bid – and by the end of the meal, we were good friends.

It makes sense in life to mend bridges with everyone you fall out with, even your worst enemies, and to try and befriend them.

Always living in the future can slow us down as much as always looking behind. Many people are always looking ahead and they never seem content. They look for quick fixes, like winning the lottery. I know that goals are important. Money is important. But the bottom line is money is just a means to an end, not an end in itself; and what is going on now is just as important as what you're planning for the future. So, even though my diary is full for months ahead, I have learned to live for the moment.

7. VALUE FAMILY AND FRIENDS

Put family and the team first
Be loyal
Face problems head on
Money is for making things happen
Pick the right people and reward talent

One evening, just up the coast from Kingston on the island of Jamaica, I sat on the beach outside a bar, listening to Bob Marley and drinking beer. In the sea, a flock of pelicans were diving after fish. They took turns, one after another, diving into shoals. They seemed to be working together so each bird would get a share. Watching them, I mused that my family was like that, a close-knit team. Virgin is also like a big family. Today, there are some 50,000 employees, but each one of them counts.

This idea of teamwork came from my childhood. Mum always tried to find something for us to do. If we tried to escape from work or responsibilities, she told us we were selfish. We did have time to play, but in her eyes, play with a purpose had more value, so instead of playing with toys, we'd ride our pony, play tennis or go bicycling. One Sunday at church instead of sitting next to a boy, who was staying with us, I slid into the seat next to my best friend, Nik. Mum was hopping mad. A guest was a guest she said, and guests must be put first. She told Dad to beat me. Instead, behind the closed door of his study he clapped his hands to make the right noise and I howled loud enough for Mum to hear. Dad was often out at work in his job as a barrister and it was Mum who was in control of the children; but they were both a big influence, and I continue to get on well with both of them today.

You can be best friends with someone and still not agree with them and, if you are close, you can get through it and remain friends. When Nik came to see what Jonny and I were up to with *Student*, he was taken aback by the way we handled money – which was chaotically, to say the least. Our 'bank' was an old biscuit tin, accessible to anybody. When we had a bill to pay, we counted the cash in the tin and not too surprisingly, often, it wasn't enough. We always seemed to be behind. I knew Nik was good at handling the money side of things, and I talked him into not taking up his place at university to join us on the magazine. He moved our cash out of the biscuit tin and into a proper bank account, bills were paid more or less on time, and some of the level of stress went down. *Student* had mostly been sold by volunteers in schools and universities, which at times could be pretty hit and miss. Crucially, Nik organised better means of distribution.

To the great relief of Jonny's long-suffering parents, he also helped find us a big house, in the heart of the West End, and we moved out of our cramped basement office. Before long, we were like a hippie commune, with up to forty of us sleeping all over the place on mattresses. The house was in my parents' names, so I thought they'd have a fit – but they even pitched in sometimes to help, and Lindi came to stay during her holidays.

I used some of our income to set up a student advisory service in the crypt of St Martin-in-the-Fields church, space we were donated, and we advised students on anything from renting flats, to VD, abortions (which were almost impossible to get, and expensive) to talking people out of suicide. It was very worthwhile and I was proud of all that we were achieving. I thought things were going well, so I was shocked when I sat down at my desk – a marble tombstone – at the Crypt one day, to find a memo to the staff from Nik that he had left there by mistake. It said that they should sack me as editor and publisher and turn *Student* into a co-op.

I felt betrayed, but knew I had to turn the crisis around by getting rid of Nik, even though he'd been my best friend for as long as I could remember. I asked him to step outside and said, 'Some of the others have come to me and said they don't like what you're planning.' I was filled with anguish, but stayed calm and acted as if I knew all about it.

Nik was in shock that he had been caught out and I could see that he didn't know what to say. I said, 'Look, *Student* is my life. We can remain friends and still see each other, but I think you should go.'

Nik looked sheepish. 'I'm sorry, Ricky,' he said. 'I thought it was for the best.'

He left to go to university and we did remain friends. It was the first real disagreement I had ever had with anyone and I was especially upset that it was with my best friend. But by facing it head on, I stopped it from getting worse. The lesson I learned was that it's best to bring things out into the open. A dispute with a friend or a colleague can be sorted in a friendly way before it escalates if you deal with it immediately.

Student continued but without Nik to keep control of our finances and distribution, our cash flow became very erratic and I knew we needed another source of income. Getting into records was almost by chance. I say almost, because although music was played constantly in our offices, I was usually too occupied on the phone and just treated it as background noise. However, I do keep my eyes and ears to the ground and saw how teenagers spent most of their disposable income on records. When the government abolished the Retail Price Maintenance Agreement – the cartel that fixed prices – record shops didn't cut prices. I instantly saw a gap and ran an ad for cut-price mail-order records in *Student*. The response was incredible.

I didn't know it, but that was to be the launch of Virgin. We handed out leaflets for mail-order records and almost overnight, we were getting sacks full of orders containing cheques and even cash. As it escalated, I saw that I couldn't do it on my own and gave Nik the chance to come back and offered him 40 per cent of the new mail-order business if he would return. He bore me no grudge and came back into the fold. Despite having got rid of the biscuit-tin system of banking, money was always tight. Nik handled the problem by cutting costs and being nice to debt collectors, who then chased us less often.

He said, 'It's fine to pay bills late, as long as you pay them in the end.'

The mail order boomed. But *Student* was taking up too much time and cash flow was always a problem because our income from our distributors took so long to come in we were always in arrears with bills and overheads. I tried to sell the magazine to IPC, one of the biggest print media groups in the UK at the time. They were eager to have me stay on as editor and asked my plans. As always, I had plenty of ideas and launched into them. I think the IPC board was stunned when they heard my lavish dreams for the future. I started talking about a cheap student bank, nightclubs and hotels for students. I said we should run a cheap train service. When I got to the cheap airline, it was clear that they thought I was a madman.

'We'll let you know,' they said as they showed me the door. 'Don't call us, we'll call you.' I often wonder what would have happened if IPC had listened to me. Would they have our airlines and trains now, instead of Virgin?

That was the end of my big plans for *Student*. In the winter of 1971 the rest of my dreams nearly came unravelled when there was a national postal strike. Our mail order business dried up overnight. Instead of waving as we went under, as many other businesses did, the long strike gave us the impetus to open our first record shop. *I had another goal.* Our enthusiasm grew, ideas flew back and forth. We wanted it to be the kind of place where students wanted to hang out, which we achieved. Our store was basic, but it had all the great records at cut prices, and we said we'd order obscure ones, at the same deal. Word of mouth is a wonderful factor and had always worked for us and it did again.

Serendipity has often played a part in my life, as when Simon Draper drifted into the Virgin offices and introduced himself as my cousin from South Africa. While he had been at university there, he had worked on the South African *Sunday Times*, so we had journalism in common; but when I heard that he was obsessed with music, and what's more showed it by talking at length on such bands as the Doors and the finer points of their lyrics, I sat up. 'Come and work for us,' I said.

He became the record buyer for the Virgin shop and the mail order list and later head of A&R for Virgin Music, signing some of our biggest successes. I told him that we only had one rule. 'What's that?' he asked.

'The Andy Williams Rule,' I said with a straight face. 'You're never ever to stock Andy Williams.'

'I think I can manage that,' he said, grinning.

Our next step was to open a recording studio. I wanted it to be a place where people could come and hang out and have fun. In those days, recording studios were mostly in London and they were run from nine to five, like an office. They were hostile places for bands to work in. Having to play rock 'n' roll at nine o'clock in the morning was not fun. Also, every band had to drag in their own gear and a selling point for us would be to supply everything they needed, from drums to amps. I decided to look for a large country house, where we could all be one big, happy family.

I was excited when I saw an ad for a castle for sale for only £2,000. It was a bargain. I loved the idea of owning a castle. I dreamed of bands like the Beatles and the Stones flocking there to record. Full of high hopes and big plans, I drove to Wales to inspect it. Sadly, the castle was stuck in the middle of a new housing estate. It had no private grounds and I knew musicians wouldn't want to go there to stay and record. My dreams faded. On the way back to London, reluctant to return empty-handed, I flicked through a glossy magazine and saw another ad for an old manor house, near Oxford. It wasn't a castle, but perhaps it would do.

I drove down narrow lanes, off the beaten track. A long drive wound off through trees with a house somewhere at the end. As soon as I saw the lovely, rambling old place, I fell in love with it. Glowing in the evening sun, it stood in its own private park. There was tons of room. The Stones and the Beatles could have a wing each! It was perfect. Excited, I called the estate agent.

'It's £35,000,' he said.

'Will you come down a little?' I asked.

'For a quick sale, you can have it for £30,000. It's a bargain.'

Perhaps it was a bargain – if you had that kind of money. I was thinking more in terms of £5,000. £30,000 was so far beyond my reach it didn't seem worthwhile trying to raise it. But I had to try and achieve my dream.

For the first time in my life, I put on a smart suit and polished my old school shoes, hoping to impress my bank into giving me a loan. Later, they told me that when they saw me in a suit and polished shoes, they knew I was in trouble. I showed them the books for the mail order business and the shop. To my shock they offered to lend me £20,000. That was a lot of money in 1971 and no one had ever lent me that much before. It gave me a real buzz and sense of pride and I strode out of the bank feeling on top of the world. I felt I had come a long way since the days – only five years ago – when I'd stood in the pay phone at school, trying to sell ads in *Student*. Back home, once the glow had faded, reality struck. £20,000 still wasn't enough.

I hoped my family might help. They had always been there for me and I appreciated then – as I still do – how vital that is when you are starting out. My parents had set up small trust funds for my sisters and me so that we would have £2,500 each when we were 30. I went to ask if I could have mine early. They agreed at once. Then Dad said, 'You are still £7,500 short. Where will you get it from?'

'I don't know,' I said.

Dad said, 'Go to lunch with Auntie Joyce. I'll tell her you're coming.'

Auntie Joyce was the aunt who had bet me ten shillings I wouldn't learn to swim. Dad had called her as he promised and told her all about my dreams for the Manor. She offered to lend me the money, to be paid back with interest when I could afford it. I started to babble my thanks but she stopped me. 'Look, Ricky, I wouldn't lend you the money if I didn't want to. What's money for, anyway? It's to make things happen. Besides,' she said with a smile, 'I know how you stick at things. You won that ten shillings, fair and square.'

I could still hear her words in my head when I went to pick up the huge key to the Manor. *Money was for making things happen.* I believed it then and I believe it now. I also knew that without my family I would not have been holding that big old iron key in my hand. What I didn't know was that Auntie Joyce didn't have £7,500 spare. She had such faith in me she had taken out a mortgage on her own house. I should add that I paid her back, every penny.

It took another thirteen years of hard work, sometimes a lot of stress, and always a lot of fun before we launched Virgin Atlantic. The years had flown by, but without the help of my family, friends and staff, it might never have happened. When we flew to New York, the plane was packed with my family and friends, all the people who counted in my life. As I looked at the proud and happy faces of my family, I knew they had helped make me what I was.

I have learned always to reward talent. Even if someone is hired to do one thing, if they have good ideas, or can handle something else, just let them do it. This is why I walk around, asking people's advice in the street, on a plane or on a train. It's true what they say – that the man in the street often has more common sense than many big bosses. Ken Berry is a good example. Ken started in one of our record shops as a clerk. His first job was to check the takings, but before long he was doing many other things. Whenever I wanted to know something, it didn't matter what, I would call Ken. He seemed to know everything about everything. Today, people turn to Google or Yahoo. We just asked Ken.

Two of the best things about him were that he could get on with people, and that he didn't have an ego. We found he was good at dealing with anyone from the top stars to their lawyers. Soon we had him handling contracts. It was obvious that his talents were wasted as a clerk and he joined our small team in running Virgin. He became CEO of Virgin Music and, some years later, when I sold Virgin to EMI he continued in that position.

I didn't always follow Ken's advice. Once, when we had expanded too fast and were running out of cash, I called a crisis meeting. At the time, our top seller was Mike Oldfield's *Tubular Bells*. Its massive sales funded everything. But our contract with Mike had expired and he was pushing for more money to renew it. I was very frank with him. I told him that the whole of Virgin Music was making less money than he was on his own.

'Why?' he asked.

I explained that we had many bands that didn't make any money at all.

'So I finance it all?' he said.

I nodded. 'Yes, pretty much.' I thought he would be pleased to learn how many bands he was helping to support.

But he looked peeved. 'I'm not giving my money away for you to blow it on a load of rubbish,' he said. 'You can afford to pay me more.'

At the crisis meeting, I said all our eggs were in one basket. We needed to sign more bands and singers. We needed more hits in order to spread the risk and increase the size of the company.

Ken Berry had been doing his sums. 'It's clear to me that we need to get rid of all our bands, apart from Mike Oldfield,' he said.

I knew we could jog along and make money with Mike Oldfield; but I was worried we would stay the same small company, and if his records stopped selling, we would sink almost without a trace. I told Ken that we needed to find a new big band – fast! I came up with a good phrase: expanding out of trouble.

To save money, we cut back to the bone. We sold our cars; we closed the swimming pool at the manor. We didn't pay ourselves. Those were easy savings. The hard ones were dropping some artists and losing staff. But we had to cut right back, to survive. We came through at last when we took a huge gamble by signing the Sex Pistols, who had been bought – and instantly sold on – by every major label, which found them too hot to handle. But they were *supposed* to behave badly; they were the start of Punk – which was the new big thing.

On an amusing note, when we dropped Dave Bedford, who wrote great music, he wrote me a very nice letter, saying he understood. It was pages long, all very friendly and polite. At the same time, he also wrote to Mike Oldfield, calling me all the vile names under the sun. It was a pity for him that he put the wrong letters in the wrong envelopes!

People have asked me how I can take so much time off to go on adventures around the world. My answer is, delegation. When you pick the right people, you can leave them to it. You know that things will run smoothly if you're not there. In 1987, I was in the middle of a boardroom battle to buy EMI, when I had to dash off. I had agreed to fly a balloon across the Atlantic with Per, and the weather was right. If we delayed, we could miss the moment. I went, knowing that I had the right people to talk the deal through. However, with the very real risk that I might die, the talks were put on ice until I returned – if I returned.

The hurricane in October of that year blew away all our dreams of owning EMI. The stock market crashed and our shares dropped in value. The banks didn't have faith that things would go up again and wouldn't lend us the money. In the end, I forgot about our takeover bid. Ironically, during the 'dirty tricks affair' with British Airways, when I was struggling to keep the airline afloat, I had to sell Virgin Music to EMI for half a billion pounds. It was one of the saddest days of my life and I can remember walking up Oxford Street after the deal had been signed, and seeing an *Evening Standard* poster by a news stand which suddenly brought it home to me, more than anything else, what I had done. 'BRANSON SELLS FOR £510 MILLION CASH.' I stumbled on, my eyes blinded with tears. But in business you have to make some very hard choices. If the airline went under, hundreds of people would lose their jobs. That billion dollars made us safe for a very long time and gave me the cash to start up new businesses. And Virgin Music was also safe. We all survived, which was the main thing.

If anyone asked me what I believe in above all else, I would say, my family. I firmly believe in the family. I know that sometimes families split up, and I have been through some of that myself. And I know that some people don't have anyone. But close friends can be like a family. We all need a strong support network. Even though I was taught to stand on my own feet, without my loyal family and friends I would be lost.

8. HAVE RESPECT

Be polite and respectful
Do the right thing
Keep your good name
Be fair in all your dealings

When I was young and impoverished, but brimming with enthusiasm and the conviction that I could achieve anything, I flew to Japan and rather ambitiously set up numerous meetings with people in the media and entertainment world. This was before Virgin Music existed, or Mike Oldfield and *Tubular Bells*, so I'm not sure what I was thinking about, or what I had to pitch to them. I think I vaguely wanted to set up some kind of joint venture to distribute records, or perhaps I was just sounding them out. They were very courteous to a broke young man in sweater and jeans and listened to me seriously in meetings where immaculate geisha girls served tea. I appreciated that and have never forgotten it.

Those patient men taught me how important it was always to keep eyes and ears open and to be polite. Japanese maxims are full of sayings like: you never know who might hear or see you. People talk. Gossip has a habit of getting back to those you gossip about.

I have come across this myself. One time I had to go to a meeting. I was late and grabbed some papers I needed to work on and jumped into a taxi. On the way, the driver got very chatty. He said, 'Oi! I know you. You're that Dick Branson. You've got a record label.'

'Yes that's right,' I said.

'Well, ain't it my lucky day. Fancy having Mr Branson in my cab.'

I hoped he might shut up so I could read my papers for the meeting, but he went on. He said he might be a cabby by day, but he was also a drummer in a band. He asked if I'd like to hear his demo tape. My heart sank. People were always playing tapes to me in the hopes they would be discovered.

But I didn't want to be rude. 'That would be lovely,' I said.

'No, you look tired. Tell you what, my mum lives around the corner. She'd love to meet you. Let's drop in and have a quick cup of tea.'

'No, I'm late–' I started to say.

'I insist, guv. A cup of tea's what you need.'

'Thank you,' I said, weakly.

Just as we reached the house, the driver put on his tape. I heard the words over the speakers, 'I can feel it, coming in the air tonight . . .' He jumped out of the front seat and held the door open for me. The cabby was Phil Collins, laughing like mad.

Japanese folklore is also full of stories of the prince in disguise, going among the peasants to see what people thought of them. When I made *The Rebel Billionaire*, I thought of that legend and the idea of being a cabby from Phil and copied it. I made myself look like an old cabby and drove the young contestants in the series to the manor house, where we would be filming. I had my ears peeled and listened to what they said in the back. I also noted how they treated an old man who couldn't lift heavy cases. I learned a lot about them, much to their dismay.

Respect is how to treat everyone, not just those you want to impress.

The Japanese can wait two hundred years for a long-term goal for their company. They don't look for the quick buck. They want slow, solid capital growth. One time, I was looking for a partner to take a stake in Virgin Music. We talked to many Americans over a period of time, sounding them out. They wanted to invest, but they also wanted to be hands on, which to them meant being closely involved in the running of the company. But we had our own way of working, so we wanted a silent partner. We knew a partner that was too hands on could cause conflict. I remembered the Japanese businessmen who had treated me so kindly a few years before, so we turned to the East. I asked the Japanese businessman who came to see me how he saw us working together.

'Mr Branson,' he asked gently, 'would you prefer an American wife or a Japanese wife? American wives are very difficult – lots of divorce and alimony. Japanese wives are very good and quiet.'

Good and quiet didn't mean weak. It sounded perfect – and we went with his company.

One of the best lessons I ever learned was when I did something illegal. I got caught and paid for it. At the time, I thought I was being a bit of a longhaired pirate. It even seemed a game. I thought I was being bold – but I was also being foolish. Some risks just aren't worth it.

During the 1970s we were all a bit hippie. The mood was very much 'us and them'. With all the other renegades, many of them now notable actors, writers, musicians and politicians, I'd gone on protest marches against Vietnam and been chased by the police, I'd waved banners and climbed up onto the plinth of Nelson's column. It was fun to protest, but we also felt passionate about the Vietnam War. (I wish we'd protested harder against the war in Iraq.) Pirate radios were blasting the airwaves from offshore. People were doing drugs by the wagonload. It was exciting.

My scam seemed a neat little trick that I convinced myself was practically legal. It started by accident in the spring of 1971. Virgin was known for selling cool, cut-price records and we had a large order from Belgium. If you exported records to Belgium, you didn't have to pay tax on them; so I bought these tax-free records direct from the big record companies like EMI and hired a van to take them across the Channel on the ferry. My plan was to land in France and drive on to Belgium. I didn't know that in France you had to pay tax, even if you were in transit on the way to somewhere else.

At Dover the Customs people stamped my papers with the number of records I had. When I arrived in France, I was asked for proof that I wasn't going to sell the records in France itself. I showed my order from Belgium and said I was just passing through France, but it did no good. The French said I had bonded stock and had to pay tax.

I was annoyed and upset because my intentions were honest and straightforward and it seemed to me that French Customs was being very stuffy, so I argued about it and they wouldn't budge. Since I didn't want to pay tax, I had to return by ferry to Dover with all the records still in the van, angry that I had wasted my time and lost a good order. But on the drive back to London, it dawned on me that I now had a vanload of tax-free records. I even had a customs stamp to prove it. I thought I could still sell them by mail order or in the Virgin shops and make about £5,000 extra profit.

It was against the law, but I just thought I was bending the rules a bit and taking advantage of a situation that wasn't of my making. After all, I had started out to do the right thing. At the time, Virgin owed the bank £15,000 and now it seemed as if luck, or fate, was helping us out. I had always got away with breaking rules and thought this was no different. I would have got away with it as well if I hadn't been greedy. Instead of just selling that one vanload and being satisfied with a windfall, I made a total of four trips to France, pretending each time that the records were for export, and turned right around again as soon as I landed on French soil, before going through their customs. The last time, I didn't even bother getting on the ferry. After I got my stamp from customs, I just drove in a circle in the port at Dover, in one gate and out the other, and headed home. I am sure that if I hadn't been stopped

I might have carried on. It was so easy. Only it wasn't easy. I was being watched.

The real problem was that I was just small fry in a far bigger scam operated by much larger record chains who were doing what I'd stumbled into by accident, but they were doing it on a far wider and more cynical scale. I was only dealing with one vanload of the records we liked and sold in our one existing shop in Oxford Street – though in all honesty, we were also going to put a few in the shop we were about to open in Liverpool. But the bigger operators had a more sophisticated system going and were distributing right across the country. I got an anonymous tip-off at midnight when I was in bed, to say that we were to be raided first thing in the morning. I was shocked by this terrifying news and listened in a sick daze as the caller explained that all the records I'd bought for export from EMI had an invisible E stamped on them that you could only see under an ultraviolet sun lamp. Before he hung up, he said he was helping me because I had helped a suicidal friend of his through the *Student* advisory service.

We had one night to get rid of all the tax-free stock. I called Nik and Tony and rushed out to buy two sun lamps from an all-night chemist. We met up at our warehouse and started pulling records out of their sleeves and shining the lamps at them. As large luminous Es stared up at us, we panicked and ran in and out of the warehouse, carrying piles of records to our van before driving through deserted streets not to hide them somewhere else, or destroy them, which would have been sane and sensible – but we actually put them in the racks of the Oxford Street shop. It made no sense whatsoever, but we had the deluded idea that Customs would only raid our warehouse and not bother with our shops. By the time six burly Customs officers, who looked as if they meant business, burst into the warehouse, I had almost recovered from my panic of the previous night. Feeling rather clever, I hid a grin as I watched them search for the illegal records – we even helped them, earnestly taking records out of their sleeves and handing them over for inspection. I didn't know that they were also raiding the shops. It was a huge shock when I was arrested, driven down to Dover and thrown into prison.

I couldn't believe it. I thought that only criminals were banged up. But, alone in that bleak cell lit by the unrelenting glare of a single bright lightbulb, it slowly dawned on me that I wasn't a hippie pirate. This wasn't a game. And I *was* a criminal. My headmaster's words came back to me. When I left school, aged sixteen, he had said, 'Branson, I predict that you will either go to prison or become a millionaire.'

I wasn't a millionaire – but I was in prison. My parents had always drummed into me that all we had in life was our good name. You could be rich, but if people didn't trust you, it counted for nothing. I lay on a bare plastic mattress with just an old blanket and vowed that I would never do anything like this again. I would spend the rest of my life doing the right thing.

In the morning, Mum came to the court to support me. I had no money for a lawyer and applied for legal aid. The judge told me if I asked for legal aid I wouldn't get bail, which he set at a whopping

£30,000. I didn't have that kind of money. I had the Manor, but it was still mortgaged, so Mum put up her home as security. Her trust in me was almost more than I could bear. She looked at me across the court and we both started to cry.

I will always remember her words on the train back to London. 'I know you've learned a lesson, Ricky. Don't cry over spilt milk. We've got to get on and deal with this head on.'

Instead of going to court, Customs agreed to settle the case by fining me a sum equal to three times my illegal profit. It came to a massive £45,000, but they said I could pay it back at the rate of £15,000 a year. It seemed a scary prospect to have to find but I wasn't angry. I had shown the law no respect and deserved to pay. Not doing anything illegal has been my watchword since then.

My way of restoring my own respect was to pay back every penny without moaning. In fact, I gained. Once again, with my back against the wall, my goal became to make a lot of money – but legally. We worked like crazy, opening new Virgin Records shops and thinking up good ideas to expand.

Ever since then, when I am asked how far I am prepared to go in achieving my aims, my answer is the same. I make it a priority not to break the law and I check all the time that I'm not.

Your reputation is everything. If you're starting in business and ask me if I have a lesson for you, I'd say, 'Be fair in all your dealings. Don't cheat – but aim to win.' This rule should extend to your private life. My motto is, 'Never do anything if you can't sleep at night.' It's a good rule to follow.

9. GAIA CAPITALISM

Leave the world a better place
Pull your weight
Take the long-term view
Always consider the implications of your actions
Big victories are made up of many small ones
Confront the big issues, they won't go away
Understand the situation then consider whether to fight
  and how
Never lose sight of the end goal
If something is wrong – fix it

In the late summer of 2006 Al Gore came to breakfast at my house in Holland Park to lay out the scenario of global warming. At the time, I didn't appreciate that what I was about to see and hear would fundamentally change the way in which I viewed the world. Three hours later, I had undergone a Road to Damascus experience.

So what was this radical lesson I had learned?

It was that if there isn't a change in carbon emissions, in a very short space of time most of the Earth will be uninhabitable.

This is such a shocking and unpalatable fact that most people deny it, or they just don't want to think about it. They believe that as individuals, they can do little about it, so push it to the back of their minds. But I can't do that. When something has to be done, we need to do it. It doesn't matter how big the challenge is or hard the solution; if I know that something is wrong, and I'm in a position to help, I will do my best to make it right.

My path to really understanding the science behind climate change has been a very long one and dates back to my old days of running *Student*, when we sat up half the night, debating practically everything. Like many people who grew up in the Sixties and Seventies, I have always been aware of environmental issues. Four of the biggest influences in terms of my view of the environment were Sir Peter Scott, founder of the WWF; Jonathon Porritt, who founded Friends of the Earth in 1984 and who is a trustee of the WWF and chairman of the Green Party; British scientist, James Lovelock; and environmental scientist and writer Tim Flannery, another good man.

Just as Virgin was getting going in 1972 and we were busy recording Virgin Records' first album, a young James Lovelock was developing a hypothesis of how the planet worked. He called this 'Gaia Theory'. He put forward with great clarity the view that the Earth was one single enormous living organism and every single part of the ecosystem reacted with every other part, even though there was no obvious link between them. He set out the theory that if any one part of the planetary system got stressed the Earth would react automatically to remove the problem. In effect, it healed itself.

The concept of Mother Earth has been a part of human culture since we first evolved and so he adopted the ancient Greek name for the Earth goddess, Ge or Gaia, for his theory. Gaia embodies Mother Earth as the source of all living and non-living entities. She is feminine and nurturing but also ruthlessly cruel. Most of the scientific community ridiculed Lovelock but, as a simple layman, I always found his ideas very attractive. Thirty years later, the same theory is almost universally accepted and forms much of the basis of our current understanding of global warming and the need to cut carbon emissions into the atmosphere before the Earth turns around and kills the problem – in this case, you and me: the human race.

We can no longer believe that our actions in one part of the planet are isolated and don't affect the planet as a whole. Deforestation, the increase of emissions of carbon dioxide, farming, pollution – even over-fishing – all have an effect on our planet. For the history of humanity, even while populations have expanded and developed, the Earth has managed to be self-regulating. But during the past century the speed of industrialisation and population growth has increased at an unprecedented pace and finally Gaia is running out of options.

I have never met James Lovelock, but I can remember debating all these issues with Jonathon Porritt, who has been a friend since the 1970s. Our discussions were more on an ecological level. We discussed such subjects as pollution, population, how to save the whale and how to grow organic food. We had no real concept of climate change until the 1990s. Overall, there was no cohesion or sense of urgency over environmental issues. For most people, ecology was something that slightly crackpot rural dwellers or the 'green' Germans and Swedes did. In many respects the Seventies was a false dawn. Conservation and animal welfare, already established causes, came together with New Age idealism and a doom and gloom scenario. Books such as *The Limits to Growth* and *A Blueprint for Survival*, which warned of an imminent planetary apocalypse caused by pollution, overpopulation and industry, became huge bestsellers. After the *Blueprint* authors were invited to address MPs, the Department of the Environment was created in 1970. It was a well-meaning idea but had little real impact.

Despite acid rain, the deforestation of the Amazon, Africa, the Philippines and New Guinea and, in 1985, the discovery of a hole in the ozone layer over the Antarctic, other political issues, such as strikes, worldwide recession and terrorism became more important. Even when Prime Minister Margaret Thatcher appointed Sir Crispin Tickell to advise on the environment and the greenhouse effect, his warning in 1989 that global warming would create refugees from the worst affected countries was practically ignored. A few people bought biodegradable toilet paper and detergent; Ecover became a brand that 'The Greens' and Paul and Linda McCartney bought; stores like Tesco's, while building on acres of greenfield sites, issued press releases to say they were 'going green'. Then it all fizzled out in the recession of the early 1990s, when people cut back on green products, which cost more. By the boom of the late 90s, we all went back to consuming more of everything.

This is where we were at, environmentally speaking, when Steve Howard, an environmental physicist who runs The Climate Group, telephoned to ask if he could bring Al Gore to breakfast. I agreed, having no real idea of how deeply I would be influenced by our discussion.

The Climate Group, which is based outside London and with offices around the world, was set up some four years ago as a not-for-profit organisation. It is funded by non-governmental organisations (NGOs) like the Rockerfeller Foundation and works very closely with the British government and individual states in the US (but not the federal government) as well as other states around the world. Its primary role is to introduce companies and governments to each other and convince them to work in a joined up way on climate change.

According to Steve, 'It was crystal clear that there was a leadership vacuum on climate change. It was everybody else's problem.' He said, 'Because of the importance of tackling global warming, business leaders who are well known around the world, like yourself, could make a difference.' His idea was to involve people who, he believed, would be listened to – but more importantly, who were in a position to lead a change. I saw this as a slower approach, rather than making a grand gesture. It was only later, because I'm in transport, that I saw how I could make a difference. Steve's first step in the UK was to host a showing of Al Gore's film on global warming, *An Inconvenient Truth*, at the IMAX cinema in London – the biggest screen in the UK – to which 400 influential people were invited. I was invited but couldn't make it so instead Steve arranged for Al Gore to come to my home.

Al is dealing with the issue of CO_2 emissions in as non-partisan a way as he can, given that he's a Democrat and the Republicans are in power as I write this. He wanted to see me because I am an operator of transport companies and he believes that the biggest initiative has to come from reducing CO_2 emissions.

It was quite an experience having a brilliant communicator like Al Gore give me a personal PowerPoint presentation. Not only was it one of the best presentations I have ever seen in my life, but it was profoundly disturbing to become aware that we are potentially facing the end of the world as we know it. The impact could be so great on humanity and the natural world that we have no choice but to do something drastic, first to stop it and then turn it around.

During our intense discussion, Steve Howard said that we need to make people confident that this was a problem that could be solved. People thought dealing with climate change could be the end of the economy and was an insoluble problem; but there is a lot we can do. We really have no choice in the matter: we *have* to do it. The Climate Group has set out to build a powerful constituency that could take that message out there and I, as a very successful businessman and communicator, could help change people's perception and drive these necessary changes.

Al agreed. Looking directly at me, he said, 'Richard, you and Virgin are icons of originality and innovation. You can help to lead the way in dealing with climate change. It has to be done from the top down, instead of from the bottom up on a grassroots level, as before.'

Grassroots does have a role to play, but I very quickly saw that there are two massive issues at stake, and while they are linked, they are different.

On the one hand, there is pollution. Pollution resonates in the environment and the natural world, as Rachel Carson showed in her book *Silent Spring* – where toxic chemicals such as weed-killers and pesticides destroyed animals, especially birds, until one day people woke up to a silent world without birdsong. Pollution fills landfill sites with rubbish and the seas with toxic chemicals. Seals and whales get mercury in their systems and coral reefs vanish. All this is tragic and horrible.

But it is CO_2 emissions that are the biggest cause of global warming – and it is global warming that will potentially change the world beyond all recognition, making it a hostile environment. *Thus, it is CO_2 emissions that we have to fix first and foremost.*

Nature does, and always has, released CO_2 into the atmosphere, but unless there is a major catastrophe – such as a mega-volcanic eruption – this has never upset the natural balance. In very simple terms, CO_2 is used by plants and converted into oxygen – all we need are trees to survive. But Al's presentation showed me that, thanks to the human species' unknowing activities and manic drive to progress, if the current trend continues the world will continue to warm at an uneven and unpredictable rate.

Already, 200 cities across the US have suffered record temperatures in the past eighteen months. You pick your place, whether it's Paris or Tokyo, and you'd find there have already been record temperatures there. There would be no respite from the heat at night, as at present, so vulnerable people in non-air-conditioned buildings would die. There'd be more extreme weather in terms of rainstorms and windstorms, which have increased radically over the past fifteen years. India would have more typhoons; there'd be massive tropical storms, hurricanes and widespread floods in places that had never experienced them on that scale before. We were looking at Armageddon.

All this was put to me in a very compelling fashion. Al Gore's lecture was a polemic, but it had enough good science around it to work really well. I think it was the first time I'd been presented with the full enormity of climate change. I found myself saying, 'I'm just about to launch a new air route to Dubai.' Usually I like doing that kind of thing – but now I can see the paradox of it. We want a connected world, we want to be able to fly, but we also must beat climate change.

'How much time do we have?' I asked.

Al said we didn't have to do all of it in ten years; but what the scientists were saying is that we may have as little as ten years before we cross a tipping point, beyond which it will be too late. We have to make a massive and determined start. If we do, it is possible to start levelling out CO_2 within the next five years. Part of our resistance to change is due to evolution. Our brains are good at perceiving danger in the form of fangs and claws and spiders and fire. It's more difficult to trigger the alarm parts of the brain – those connected to survival – with grave dangers that can only be perceived through abstract models and complex data – in other words, dangers that can't be seen until too late.

That was one of the big problems in some of the early phases of the environmental movement of the 1970s. Armageddon was predicted by the year 2000, but it never happened. The phrase 'doom and gloom' was born, and people just switched off. They didn't get upset when oil companies stopped investing in renewable energy, which they were doing in the Seventies because the oil price went down. There was no political will to do anything about it among the general population. In fact the general population had got a little bit scared by some of these predictions and I think that still remains the case today. If you are told you are bad and you are doing something bad, it just creates a blame culture: it's not my fault, it's the Chinese; it's not my fault, it's the Americans; it's the big companies; it's aviation; it's cars – and so forth. We're not going to create a different industrial climate and social climate when people just blame someone else. The blame culture is very negative. I believe that we should take a much more *fun* approach to things. Yes, we must change the way we live, but that doesn't mean we have to stop having fun.

A lot of the debate over the environment has been based on politics and hasn't been based on science, though it has moved much more towards science since 2000. I believe that we need to develop science and the need for an industrial response to it, as opposed to a change of lifestyle. As Jonathon Porritt says, 'I've seen a few too many of these green enthusiasm spikes. The environment can't spend another thirty years going in and out of fashion.' He's right. If I go and live on a farm in the west coast of Scotland, and grow organic vegetables and have a little wind-powered plant, I'm not going to feed two million people in the UK or make much of a contribution to reducing global carbon. But industry and business with their massive resources can and must do this.

People just don't like being fed doom and gloom stories. They want to get on with their lives and see no reason to change – and they say things like, 'What's wrong with a little extra sunshine, anyway? People pay good money to sit in the sun on holiday, don't they?'

As Andrew Simms, policy director at the New Economics Foundation has said, 'A huge gap is emerging between awareness of global warming and action to deal with it. We're behaving like a group of people agreed that the building around us is on fire, but unwilling to reach for the alarm or the fire extinguisher.'

Now that I knew what was at stake, I couldn't be one of those refusing to reach for the fire extinguisher. It seemed to me that there were powerful lessons to be learned – not only for me, but for us all. We can all play a part, either directly on a governmental and business level, or indirectly by pushing for change through politics and pressure groups.

Sitting down with Will Whitehorn, Virgin Group's Corporate and Brand Development Director, we carefully discussed these issues and took the decision to change the way Virgin operates on a corporate and global level. We called this new Virgin approach to business Gaia Capitalism in honour of James Lovelock and his revolutionary scientific view. Along with our branded venture capital way of doing business, I believe it will help Virgin to make a real difference in the next decade and not be ashamed to make money at the same time. It has become one of my goals to make Gaia Capitalism a new way of doing business on a global level.

I agreed to join the Climate Group's leadership council, alongside people like Al Gore and the petroleum group, BP. A petrol company might seem an anomaly, but BP is concerned enough about the future to have been engaged in this issue for a long time. A few months later, I found myself in California, with a group of political and business leaders like Tony Blair, Al Gore and Governor Arnold Schwarzenegger, for a discussion on climate change. The central message we faced was that this is a very serious issue to which an urgent response is required. It's on a scale that we're not used to dealing with, but now that we have the knowledge we can't evade responsibility to act. Doing nothing and continuing on our merry way is not an option. We have to try to put the world on a low evolution, low carbon pathway. It's about action now. It's about momentum and enthusiasm and not waiting for a year's time to have that meeting. In politics and business there is something known as an 'action gap'. This means that people talk and talk – but do nothing. We intend to do something.

During our discussions, Al Gore said, 'Lovelock is truly a visionary. But he thinks that the planet has gone beyond the tipping point. I don't agree. We can reduce carbon emissions to a point where nature is in balance again.'

I believe there is a hunger to be part of a larger vision that changes the way we relate to the environment and the economy. Right now, the US is borrowing huge amounts of money from China to buy huge amounts of oil from the most unstable region of the world, and to burn it in ways that destroy the habitability of the planet. That is nuts! We have to change *every aspect* of that.

Eighteen years ago, Jonathon Porritt co-wrote a book called *The Coming of the Greens*. It concluded with a discussion of what Jonathon called the brinkmanship theory. He wrote:

> Only when a major catastrophe looms will the necessary international cooperation, awareness and solidarity be forthcoming. There is some hope in such a strategy, but it entails high risks. By the time we get to the brink, the momentum and systemic inertia which took us there may well be too strong to reverse.

Al Gore said that he thought Hurricane Katrina was a tipping point for millions of Americans. Recently a top insurance executive at Lloyd's of London said that if we don't act now to prevent this looming catastrophe, 'the population of the world will face extinction'. It's a sophisticated debate between the geologists on one side and the economists on the other. But the debate over oil reserves misses the point. We have more than enough oil, not to mention coal, to completely destroy the habitability of the planet. As I write, China and America have said they will continue to mine coal for at least a further fifty years. The real constraint on oil and coal is not supply, but global warming. There's a saying: 'The Stone Age didn't end because we ran out of stones.'

And the Age of Fossil Fuels won't end because we run out of fossil fuels. Something else will take its place. We have to ensure that that something won't cause our extinction.

According to Gore, 'The fact that oil is beginning to get more expensive more quickly will contribute to the realisation of how dysfunctional our current pattern is. Take the tar sands of western Canada. For every barrel of oil they extract there, they have to use enough natural gas to heat a family's home for *four* days. And they have to tear up four *tons* of landscape, all for one barrel of oil. It is truly nuts. But you know, junkies find veins in their toes. It seems reasonable, to them, because they've lost sight of the rest of their lives. As Lincoln said in the darkest days of America's darkest passage: "We must disenthrall ourselves, and then we shall save our country." Our biggest challenge, our biggest foe, is thrall. The word sounds ancient, but it means anything that imprisons our thinking and prevents us from seeing the reality of our situation. We're in thrall to oil. We've got to break out of it. We must disenthrall ourselves, and then we will save our planet.'

Even before I talked to Al Gore, many omens were already coming together to make me sit up and pay attention. Virgin's fuel bill went up by half a billion dollars between 2004 and 2006, which is a lot of money, enough to make us pause. Research showed us that this was mostly due to a shortage of capacity. For whatever the reason, oil companies are not investing in oil refineries. Also, OPEC has a stranglehold over the amount of fuel that's sold. There isn't an organisation on the side of the consumer that's trying to counter this degree of control and neither are our governments doing much about it. The end result is that, from airline tickets to driving in cars, prices are rising. This could lead to a recession.

My initial reaction was to say, 'Let's build an oil refinery.'

We looked into it and when we realised the huge cost, we thought of joining forces with other airlines, cruise companies and others that are affected by this to see if we could get a few oil refineries built. We were still thinking about this when Al Gore came to talk to me and I saw that global warming was a greater problem. This is when I first started to wonder if there was a way in which we could actually drive fuel prices down, but at the same time help the environment.

Much of this has caught people on the hop because we're used to the environment being 'over there' and suddenly it's a mainstream issue. It's actually an economic issue, a social issue, a development issue, a human rights issue that touches all aspects of how and who we are. Over the next few decades we've got to change our transport systems, change our energy systems, change aspects of production on a global level. We must make significant changes over time so that we can beat air pollution and reduce fuel poverty. There are many ways we can go about this. Decentralising power is one, so that food sources and manufacturing plants are close to the people they serve. Another is to change the kind of fuel we use. It doesn't have to be a sacrifice – in fact, some of it is a very attractive proposition. If we don't respond to this challenge we will have a society that is difficult to sustain.

George Orwell wrote, 'We human beings are capable of convincing ourselves of something that's not true long after the accumulated evidence would convince any reasonable person that it's wrong.' We have to keep that collision with reality from happening with the climate crisis, because by the time the worst consequences begin to unfold, it will be too late.

This is what led to my joining Bill Clinton, Rupert Murdoch and Al Gore in New York, a group that the media termed a climate change juggernaut, to personally pledge $3 billion to develop biofuels. My promise was a firm commitment, intended not just to move the Virgin group forward, but to inspire others. The idea is to pinpoint our transport companies as funding this investment, but if it's not met from that direction, the money will come out of our existing businesses. By reason of direct linkage and principle we are going to do this investment programme, whatever it takes. What is the point of holding back when there will be no businesses? When people will be fighting for a square yard on which to live, somewhere in France or Switzerland?

After my public announcement, which within moments was beamed around the world, Steve Howard said, 'Richard, we work with lots of different organisations, but the pace of change at Virgin is without parallel. It is really impressive to see the Virgin machine unleash itself.'

My answer was, we can and will do as much as we can to lead from the front by example. It's a learning curve for business as well as for people. If every individual person in the world makes even a small change to the way they live, it will be like a huge tidal wave. We can walk or bicycle like the Dutch instead of driving the kids to school. Lights can be switched off, the heating turned down a couple of degrees (we used to wear sweaters when it was cold; now people sit around in their overheated houses in T-shirts), houses can be insulated and solar panels installed and so on. All these are obvious. On a wider scale, we need to persuade countries with vast swathes of forest not to cut them down. It's not even a matter now of saving endangered species or wondering why fish are off the menu. It's a matter of survival. The Amazon rainforest has been described as the 'lungs of our planet' because it continuously recycles carbon dioxide into oxygen – more than 20 per cent of the world's oxygen is produced there. Rainforests are microclimates. Evaporation from the trees turns into rain; the moisture is recycled. When the trees are gone, places like Brazil will be deserts, less oxygen will be produced for the world and all the CO_2 currently trapped in the soil will be released into the atmosphere.

At least 80 per cent of the developed world's diet originated in the tropical rainforest. Leaving the rainforests intact, and harvesting their fruits and medicinal plants, has more economic value than the return from timber or grazing land for cattle. If managed properly, the rainforest can provide the world's need for these natural resources on a perpetual basis. Even as I write this, I am aware that one and a half acres of rainforest are lost every second – with tragic consequences for both developing and industrial countries. It is estimated that by the year 2020 the last remaining rainforests could be gone.

One of the most obvious ways of stopping this deforestation is for the West to pay forest nations to not cut down their trees.

Europe already does this with agricultural land. Farmers are paid to not use their land. It's called set-aside. It makes better sense to 'set aside' the great rainforests of the world. It will be cheaper in financial and human terms than having to deal with the consequences.

It is a huge challenge because – just looking at the undeveloped world, and to places like China and India – we have to recognise that they want to catch up with the West. In fact, despite the justifiable accusations levelled against them in regard to pollution, they already have green targets in place for renewable energy. There are more wind farms off Bangladesh, for example, than anywhere else in the world. Asia has more wind energy, more solar thermal, more hot water, than anywhere else on the planet; but they're also in a rush for development. They have an ageing population in China and they want to get rich before they get old. They have 50 million people, who still haven't got access to electricity, and you can't try and stop them, but it has to be done in a more efficient way – and they recognise that. It's a huge challenge and there are some paradoxes. It's like the birth of the industrial revolution in the Far East, with their coal-fired power stations producing so much CO_2. On the other hand, neither the US nor Australia will sign up to Kyoto, and the US is the biggest carbon polluter of all.

I want to pass on some of the lessons I have learned and in order to be more informed, I have studied the science and taken advice from experts.

To some extent I am following James Lovelock's model. He says that CO_2 reduction is the trigger of energy efficiency; not reducing the gas or electricity bill or growing organic vegetables. One modern environmental scientist I am learning from is the Australian Tim Flannery, who wrote a groundbreaking book, *The Weathermakers*. An internationally acclaimed scientist, explorer and conservationist, his books include the definitive ecological histories of Australia. As a field zoologist he has discovered and named more than thirty new species of mammals – or as someone said, 'he has discovered more species than Charles Darwin'. He has said, 'The climate is the great regulator of life on Earth, and our climate is on the cusp of changing swiftly.'

When someone with his credentials says something, you have to pay attention. I invited him to speak to all managing directors of Virgin worldwide on environmental science. I think what Tim will do for us is give the scientific background to the path we've now embarked on. It is not just about having green credentials. I have made a firm commitment that this is going to be an industrial strategy for Virgin in the twenty-first century.

It's brave in a sense because we're going to get a lot of criticism for it. I can hear people saying, 'If CO_2 emissions are the problem, why doesn't Richard Branson just stop his planes from flying?' But it doesn't make sense in this day and age. People want to fly and somebody else would just fill the gap who might have no sense of responsibility at all. We want to be the people who fly, but in a responsible way. One of these ways is to try to find an entirely new low carbon fuel for aviation, but we're a long way from that. Aviation fuels put 2 per cent of the world's CO_2 emissions into the atmosphere. This doesn't sound a lot, but on a global scale, every reduction in the total counts. Fuels like bioethanol exist for ground transportation, made from biomass (using vegetable matter, such as sugar or maize) but it's a stopgap. One of the problems is that replacing the world's requirements of petroleum oil with biofuel would use up the whole world's agricultural output. We'd have enough fuel, but we wouldn't be able to feed ourselves.

Another problem is that ethanol can't be pipelined, because it picks up water that rusts the pipe. It can only come to blending stations by truck, train, or barge. The main concentration of Virgin's effort and investment is going to be on searching for entirely new fuels for the future: finding a new fuel for aviation and the best and most efficient fuel for ground transport. This new fuel hasn't been invented yet and I admit that we're feeling our way to some extent. Our plans might not even be successful, but we have to try, even though it is not the most cost-effective way forward for a capitalist enterprise like Virgin. But money and profit are not the issue.

One biofuel we're looking at is butanol. In order of energy efficiency, butanol is at the top end of the biofuels, while ethanol is at the bottom end. Butanol can be used in ordinary existing car engines but the most efficient way to produce ethanol or butanol is by using cellulosic methods – that's when you use all the biomass, or cellulose, of the plant, the parts you usually throw away, like stalks and straw – and we're still five years away from making that commercially viable with butanol.

Initially, given current technology, we're going for some straightforward bioethanol investments with a twist. My philosophy is to be economical with the method of production, including transport. At the moment, huge tankers carry oil around the world. Shipping produces far more CO_2 than aeroplanes, so this makes no sense. I want to produce fuels in the area, or close to, where they will be used. Most of the ethanol in America at the moment is produced in the Mid West and transported in very expensive tankers to the oil majors to mix it with fuel, with the best going to the East Coast. California produces virtually no ethanol of its own and its biofuel is shipped in from the east. So we are building an ethanol plant powered by wind right beside the railhead that carries the corn to the cattle industry that feeds California with its dairy produce and its beef. We will make fuel and use the residue to sell to the farmers for their cattle. This seems logical, yet logic has rarely come into it where the oil industry is concerned. Britain and Europe don't yet grow enough maize for Virgin to establish similar railhead plants here.

One of our most innovative ideas is to give a \$25 million prize to the person who can find the best way of dequestrating carbon out of the earth's atmosphere. We're looking for a method that will remove at least one billion tonnes of carbon per year from the atmosphere. The prize will be overseen by a panel of judges including Al Gore, James Lovelock and NASA scientist James Hansen. It's a very exciting challenge and, I believe, the best way to find a solution to the problem of climate change.

* * *

There are always people who criticise, and usually they're the ones who come up with no solutions. People who want to use only wind and wave also say we have to stop travelling. They refuse to consider biofuel or nuclear power. Are they aware that there are dozens of old nuclear-powered container ships still circling the world?

Ironically, Jonathon Porritt fell out with James Lovelock over nuclear fuel. Lovelock is a believer that we have to go nuclear, while Jonathon opposes it on every front. But we have done a lot of analysis and I believe that if you look at the history of nuclear and how safe it is relative to everything else that we could do in the short term, then it seems to be one of the best ways forward. It's a lot for us to swallow, living in an industrial world, but we must think seriously about building safe and secure nuclear power stations.

I have even discussed on a 'what if' level the feasibility of building small local nuclear power stations. In the 1940s and 1950s nuclear cars, planes, trains were on the agenda. Scientists had learned a lot from putting nuclear power plants into ships and with marine diesel being the biggest cause of transport pollution now, it makes sense to study going totally nuclear in container tankers. However, as technology stands, ships are about the smallest item where there's a safe and viable approach to the nuclear vehicle. We're not going to find a nuclear solution unless the biggest industrial organisations from the West get fully engaged in the new generation approach to that and are able to overcome the public resistance.

The fact is we live on a nuclear planet. We don't have to look very far down into the mantle to find it's entirely nuclear. From the dawn of time, we as a species have been massively influenced by nuclear emissions – any mammalian species is. The ground we walk on, the food we eat and the air we breathe, as well as cosmic radiation, contain small amounts of radioactivity and life forms have absorbed this into their biomasses and genetic makeup. Natural sources of radiation make up 82 per cent of the average dose people are exposed to annually, while nuclear power makes up less than one per cent.

The concept of Gaia Capitalism is all about solutions. We are taking an apparent contradiction and showing that it works and makes real sense. Virgin is like a massive ecosystem. The separate parts are separately run and managed, and even have their own shareholders, but there's always the linkages between them. Sometimes it's the brand that acts as a linkage; and sometimes the linkage is commercial. But the unique ability we have at Virgin is to keep the dialogue going between the entities while letting them get on with what they're doing in their specialist areas – as is the case with our research and development into biofuels.

Henry Ford and Rudolf Diesel never intended cars to use gasoline. When Henry Ford told a *New York Times* reporter that ethyl alcohol was 'the fuel of the future' in 1925, he believed it. 'The fuel of the future is going to come from fruit like that sumac out by the road, or from apples, weeds, sawdust – almost anything,' he said. 'There is fuel in every bit of vegetable matter that can be fermented. There's enough alcohol in one year's yield of an acre of potatoes to drive the machinery necessary to culti-vate the fields for a hundred years.'

Unbelievably, not only was Henry Ford's first Model-T built to run on fuel made from hemp, but the car itself was constructed from hemp. I don't know if Henry Ford got 'as high as a kite' – but he was frequently photographed among his hemp fields on his large estate. *Popular Mechanic* magazine wrote in 1941 that the Model-T was grown from the soil and had hemp plastic panels whose impact strength was ten times stronger than steel. Diesel, the inventor of the diesel engine, designed it to run on vegetable and seed oils like hemp. In fact he even ran it on peanut oil for the 1900 World's Fair. I was very interested to learn that a hemp crop grows faster than a forest and produces up to four times more cellulose per acre than trees. Back in the 1920s in the US there were many bills proposing a National Energy programme that made use of America's vast agricultural resources, but they were killed by smear campaigns launched by the petroleum lobby. They even used the ability to tax petrol by claiming that the US government's plans 'robbed taxpayers to make farmers rich'. If the Feds hadn't banned hemp crops in the 1930s instead of petrol, cars might have still been running safely and in an environmentally friendly way on marijuana. Now, there's a thought for the old hippies of the world.

I fervently believe that transport companies like ours have a duty not only to develop the most energy and environmentally efficient futures for our existing businesses but also to invest in the future sources of renewable energy and fuel that could make such a difference to securing the technological and industrial future of Western society.

We are looking at every future transport technology and the fuels of the future to feed those technologies but we have also had quite a lot of fun doing it. A couple of years ago, we had the chance to team up with my old friend Steve Fossett to build a revolutionary aircraft, the Virgin Atlantic Global Flyer.

It wasn't made of metal but instead it used carbon composite and was very light but capable of operating safely at very high altitudes to improve fuel efficiency dramatically. The plane is now in the Smithsonian Museum at Dulles Airport in Washington but before it went there, Steve successfully flew it around the world on less fuel per hour than a four-wheel-drive SUV uses every day taking the kids to school.

As a result we have embraced the dichotomy of being a transport operator investing in a green future. The programme will even involve space – the final frontier. Without space, and the work of organisations such as NASA, we would not even know or understand the realities of climate change. Without space we could not feed the current population of the world. Space also provides the answer to necessary future travel without atmospheric impact. However, sadly, space launch technology is still in the dirty, polluting and carbon-intensive Cold War era and there has been no private investment in viable space launch systems using renewables. We aim to change that as well.

The future may not be as green as any of us would like but if actions are taken now across the corporate world in Europe, the USA and the Far East, mankind may at least survive the turbulent hundred years we have ahead. By making green investment a motive for success rather than a charitable adjunct to companies' existence, humanity will dramatically increase the chance of its survival.

We all have to pull our weight and work hard to leave the world a better place. This is the single biggest lesson to be learned if we are – quite literally – to save the world.

10. SEX APPEAL

Be passionate about the brand and make it sexy
Use the normal to engage the enemy, the extraordinary
  to win
Walk the talk
Create excitement in everything you do
If something needs doing, do it yourself
Look beyond the obvious and put your ass on the line

I was dangling, apparently stark naked, from a crane, high above Times Square in New York, with the cast of Broadway's *The Full Monty,* also apparently naked, dangling alongside me. In fact we were wearing 'nude' bodysuits, our creative parts covered by a Virgin cellphone. It was yet another outrageous stunt to launch a new product – in this case, Virgin Mobile in the United States – and, as usual, I was the focus of attention, the very visible, public face (or in this case, body) of the brand.

My marketing people had seized on Virgin Mobile's motto, 'nothing to hide', to emphasise that our service has no hidden costs, and decided that doing the 'Full Monty' over one of the most famous places in the world – Times Square – would really shout out the message. I have been shouting out the message ever since Freddie Laker advised me to do so when we launched Virgin Atlantic in 1984. He basically told me I had to, because if I was going to fight the political battles against state-owned monopoly airlines, and big domineering American ones, there had to be a face to the brand. We would be competing with the likes of hugely rich companies like Pan Am, TWA, British Airways, but we had used all our resources on just one plane and didn't have the advertising or the spend to get ourselves noticed.

Freddie said to me, 'Richard, I know you're not actually that good at public speaking, but you've got to get out there and use yourself to try to put Virgin on the map. Try to make sure you get on the front pages, not the back pages.'

It might have been easier just to hire a public relations company and assign to them the task of publicity, but I believe that Freddie was right – I had to do it myself. So for a number of years I would do all sorts of mad things to get Virgin on the front pages, including plastering the Virgin name all over stratospheric balloons in which I went off on some pretty amazing challenges. In the name of fame and for the sake of the brand, I ended up being plucked out of the sea by helicopters; dressing in a frilly wedding gown to publicise our shops, Virgin Bride; wearing a plaid miniskirt and long blond wig as Axl Rose, the lead singer in Guns N' Roses at the opening of a new Virgin Megastore in Los Angeles; walking the plank between two balloons and bungee jumping 300 feet over the Victoria Falls and dozens more madcap exploits – all of which happened to be rather fun. I know I tend to infuriate the marketing experts because I break nearly all of their sacred rules. Alycia de Mesa, a marketing consultant and author of *Before the Brand*, said, 'You're not supposed to "stretch" a brand so much, but Richard Branson is a billionaire because he hasn't accepted limitations.'

I always tell all budding entrepreneurs, 'Whatever your field, you must be passionate about it and create excitement in everything you do. Beat your drum and look beyond the obvious.'

Virgin works hard at developing its image, from its distinctive, uplifting logo, to the way in which the businesses are presented. Entrepreneurs are people – and they don't have to become pompous or boring just as soon as they're behind a desk. I fully believe that the presentation and image of one's business should reflect the fun as well as the hard work behind it. In my view, there are no limitations on what is possible or what should be attempted. I will stretch the normal parameters every time because there's so much competition, you have to stand out from the herd. Our customers are the kind of people who are bright and innovative. As far as I am concerned, anything, however outlandish, that generates media coverage reinforces my image as a risk taker who challenges the establishment.

Another lesson I have learned is that you've got to stretch to grow. I will get involved in a new business if I think it will be fun, but it also has to pay its way. I believe that the time to go into a new business is when the genre is abysmally run by other people, and when

I feel that Virgin can provide a significantly better customer experience.

I tell people who ask me about starting up a new business forum that a question they should ask themselves is, 'Is there room for me, and can I do better?' Cell phones are an example of how I entered a crowded marketplace in a field I wasn't familiar with because I believed that I could find a niche. I admit that for many years I have resisted using a cell phone but now I have a Blackberry, which I have come to see as a necessity. It has certainly given me some freedom to move around and get out and meet people. But I realised that many young people couldn't afford the expensive monthly charges the established companies required and quickly saw that a pay-as-you-go approach would work best for teenagers and students. We'd already offered this system in the UK, but it was a novel idea for a cellular service in the United States and to really push ourselves as an innovative and youthful company, we offered features that would make our cellphones more playful, such as VoiceMania (voicemail greetings from celebrities such as William Shatner and Adam West), Rescue Rings (to save yourself from a bad blind date or a boring meeting), wake-up calls, ringtones from the latest hit songs, and music news and celebrity gossip from MTV. But I knew that the Virgin brand wasn't yet widely recognised in America – hence finding myself doing the Full Monty over Times Square. Our risqué marketing led to the *Wall Street Journal* giving us an award for the worst ad of the week.

Dan Schulman, the man I backed to start Virgin Mobile USA, gleefully accepted the award, telling our marketing team, 'The last publication I want endorsing our ads is the *Wall Street Journal*. Your goal for the fourth quarter is to win that award again.'

In the early days we ran out of cash and Dan called me to say he needed more money to order phone handsets to sell during the holiday season. I didn't hesitate and told him that I was selling La Residencia in Majorca, one of my favourite hotels in the world to fund him. Later, Dan told me, 'Richard, you won me over right there. You put your money and actions behind your words. There is nothing I or the team won't do for you.'

As far as I am concerned, the happy convergence of daredevil and publicist originates with my love of challenges and adventure. I wanted to be the first to cross the Atlantic and the Pacific in a balloon or to win the Blue Riband in a boat and, at the same time, it helped put the Virgin name on the map.

I have taken an interest in our advertisements, and the design of our logos since the 1970s. That uplifting red tick that is incorporated in the 'V' of Virgin is a great brand. The lovely thing about it is it hasn't gone through a massive transmogrification. It always makes my blood boil when I see unnecessary changes to old established and well-loved images, costing millions. I belong to the school of if it's not broken, don't fix it.

Another great brand is the one we devised for Virgin Galactic. One day, I was walking through the office when Ashley Stockwell, brand marketing director of the Virgin Group, suddenly produced a camera and snapped a close-up of my eye. He said nothing, but later handed the photograph to Philippe Starck, the most famous and prolific designer of iconic objects alive today. I heard nothing for a while, and then after a couple of months, Philippe and I met Burt Rutan, the man who had designed the Virgin Atlantic Global Flyer and who was now part of Virgin Galactic, at Necker. Philippe showed us the complete collection of remarkable logos he had designed for the Galactic project, based around a nebula, combining a human eye with its pupil. With a smile, he pointed to the blue one. 'That's yours, Richard.'

Philippe said he had chosen it because the curiosity and adventure of the human spirit exists in the vision of the human eye, through millions of years of evolution, right back to the beginning of mankind. The nebulous iris represents the infinite possibilities of this endeavour and signifies our opportunity to look back at earth from space with our own eyes for the first time. The eye's pupil incorporates an eclipse, the dawning of something new, something unique but accessible. Something far, but near.

Philippe had even drawn a futuristic vision of our first space station in New Mexico; the entire eye logo, with a blue iris and a black pupil made the top of an enormous underground silo that would open just like a James Bond film.

As I looked at the logo I was reminded of childlike awe. Whether people be six or sixty, I thought they would see that a new chapter in space flight had begun. It means a great deal to me that my parents, who will be in their nineties, will be going into space with me and my children – so three generations will be represented.

The last time I had a direct idea for advertising was with Virgin Mobile in the UK. I've known Kate Moss ever since she signed up with a model agency when she was fifteen years old, and she had become a good friend of our family. When she went through a rough patch and went into rehab, there was the usual stuffy corporate reaction and she was dropped by many of her clients. I thought it very unfair when she had done the right thing by going into rehab, and was a good role model for young people. I decided to help her and called James Kydd the marketing manager at Virgin Mobile and asked what he thought. I said that she is an extremely talented model and since she had lost all her advertising contracts, perhaps we should see if we could sign her up. I also thought that her agency would not be charging her normal fees and this would be a very good opportunity for us to grab someone of her calibre. Clearly we had to make the script really funny and really engaging to get Kate to agree to reference the issues that had sent her to rehab at the time. James briefed the advertising agency to come up with a humorous script with the angle that having lost all her contracts she can only get a pay-as-you-go phone to call her friends. The joke was her agent saying. 'Kate, baby, we've got you a new contract' – a fashion house contract – and she smiles enigmatically because she signed our Virgin Mobile contract without involving the agent.

I don't like stuffy or pompous ads, and Kate is a very good sport. She also happened to look stunning, barefooted in a fawn cashmere sweater and minuscule shorts, saying almost nothing, while her inept agent talked a mile a minute. Kate loved the storyboard and within a week we had signed her up to be the face of our 2005–2006 mobile phones campaign, that was launched at Christmas 2005.

Sales figures showed we were right, so much so that we went on to do similar tongue in cheek campaigns with Christina Aguilera, Busta Rhymes and Pamela Anderson, where to a certain extent they're also laughing at themselves. This makes the ads more engaging to the consumer and at the end of it, they like what we have to offer.

I believe in using sex appeal to promote the Virgin image and, with that in mind, we asked Pamela Anderson from *Baywatch* to be the total image of Virgin Cola – literally. In 1995 I suggested that we should do a bottle like the iconic Coke contour bottle, but in the shape of a woman, which was far more difficult than one might think it is. Ashley Stockwell and James Kydd managed to pull it of and saved the day. It was inspired by Pamela, so she signed it and we called it 'The Pammy'. We also decided, in the spirit of sexual equality, to do one with a very slim male person, in the shape of Jarvis Cocker from the band Pulp, which we wanted to call 'Cocker Cola', but Jarvis said no in the end.

I have always been very positive about doing photo shoots, sometimes in the most trying conditions. For example, when we launched Virgin Cola USA, one series with 'Evel' Knievel was shot in New York on an incredibly cold day. I can remember shivering for some fourteen or fifteen hours in the biting wind, but remaining cheerful – after all, everyone else was also shivering, including Knievel in his leathers. He turned to me at one point and quite dryly said, 'Yep, I earned fifty million dollars, but I spent fifty-one.'

It was so cold that when an attractive young woman offered me a massage to warm me up of course I accepted at once. I can remember another Virgin Cola campaign, where I did the classic things for the press, like picking up Pamela and turning her upside down. The photographers couldn't keep their eyes off her nature-defying breasts that flipped right out. I have to say that she was a very good sport about it.

If anyone asks me to advise them about promotion and branding, perhaps for a new company they want to set up, I always tell them, be true to your product. Don't make it something it's not. Take a good look at the image you want to promote and go along with that.

In our case, we won't use celebrities to say, 'Hello, we think this is a really good product.' It always seems fake to me, and doesn't reflect our image at all. We tend to do something different, preferring to use them in a little story where the schema almost comes through the celebrity not taking themselves too seriously. Ninety-nine per cent of corporations feel they have to get celebrities cooing at the product, saying how fantastic it is, but that is rather an outdated approach in my opinion and not fun or even honest.

In the early days of Virgin I used to obsess over advertising. I disliked the style then in fashion, where people would rave that the planes were so good you won't want to get off. I wanted to make people laugh. I used to be very hands on, but as the companies grew, I tended to leave the marketing people to it. But one day in 1993, I happened to be watching television and I thought I'd look at our new Virgin Atlantic commercial. I was aghast when I saw an incredibly chauvinistic ad with our cabin crew stuffing grapes into the faces of pinstriped city types. I thought it was very disrespectful to the cabin crew by suggesting that they flaunted themselves in an unseemly way, rather than care about service. The advertisement had cost an awful lot of money but it was not the image we wanted for Virgin. It was the classic way that a traditional advertising agency would approach a transport brand by overstating everything to such a degree that it wasn't very believable. I was sure that to a certain extent it would undersell the real product that Virgin had. The promotion was called 'How to Get Ahead in Business' – but I can remember thinking, 'not on my planes!'

Picking up the phone, I made a rare intervention and called Ashley Stockwell, our marketing director. We talked it through and I said I would like the ad pulled at once and was it possible to shoot another one in double-quick time?

Ashley in turn called James Kydd and said, 'We've got this terrible ad which Richard wants pulled. We've got to sort out a new one as soon as possible.'

We got rid of the agency that did the grape ad and hired a new agency to show Virgin planes in a way that was amusing without being meaningless. The result was the Terence Stamp campaign, the first of which showed him and Helen Mirren, overlaying the entire schema with sharp and funny humour, asking the question: 'Would you prefer to travel normally – or would you prefer to travel in an aeroplane which has got a bar in it?' They were very nicely shot, engaging films and instantly sales went up by about 20 per cent.

In 2006, when we were planning to launch Virgin America in the United States, I asked Fred Reid, former president of Delta, if he would like to run our proposed new carrier. I told him that I would get out there and help him shout about it. An airline is a very high profile way of getting a brand established in a marketplace and we could use all the publicity around the new airline to bolster my other American ventures. But even with using my image to help get the message out there, promotion is not cheap. We budgeted about $200 million for start-up marketing in the US.

I know that not everyone has this kind of money, nor do they have airlines; but I started very small, with no budget at all for promotion when we launched Virgin Music in the 1970s. We had some good ideas for promotion and brilliant designs. I have already mentioned the Virgin 'tick' logo; but as just one other example, we are still using one of our original grassroots Roger Dean psychedelic logos from Virgin Music circa 1973 to launch Virgin Digital. The original Virgin Music designs – which included the famous 'Gemini' logo – were Roger's first commissioned work straight from art school. He went on to be one of the top two designers from the era – Peter Blake who designed the iconic *Sergeant Pepper* record sleeve was another. The revived illustration feels entirely at home in Virgin Megastores and passes the 'Does it look cool on a T-shirt?' test. And as Darren Whittingham, Executive Creative Director at Start, the agency we used for the campaign, told me, 'It is rare these days to implement a concept so true to its original proposal. This is an idea that was right from the start.'

We wanted the UK launch campaign for Virgin Digital to pivot around a rock 'n' roll identity, from people as passionate about music as their customers.

For this reason, a lot of the promotion was done in Virgin Megastores, where banners enabled audiences to get an instant Virgin Digital 'music experience'. Virgin Digital's positioning statement, 'The world's deepest collection of music downloads', emphasises our extraordinary music credentials, with songs from 15,000 record labels. As Ashley Stockwell was to say, 'Virgin was the label of many influential bands that changed the face of music. Now we have a brand to change the face of digital music.'

At Virgin we want to create the most respected brand in the world, something to aspire to. But a brand is only as good as your products, and often that means being very well looked after. If people have a good experience on our planes or on our trains, or if they can get straight through to our people on Virgin Mobile, then they'll try the next product that we launch. It could be anything – and indeed, we do have a whole range of things they might want to try, including vodka and wine, credit cards and health clubs and much more. With 350 Virgin branded companies worldwide, if we offend one person by a bad experience or sloppy service, then we've potentially lost hundreds of customers. A brand is something that is built over many years and it's very important to get it right.

My adventurous side means that I don't get stuck behind a desk. I make sure that I spend most of my time out and about, talking to people, asking questions, making notes, experiencing my businesses through the customer's eyes. If I'm on a Virgin plane anywhere in the world I have my notebook in my pocket. I meet and talk to and listen to all the staff and crew. I shake the hands of all the passengers when they get on board the plane and when we're in the air I leave my seat and wander about, chatting. If you meet five hundred passengers on a regular basis, as I do, you'll be told about any little details that are not right. By following through, I hope to build an exceptional airline or an exceptional train-line. I also write to every one of those business-class passengers who write to me, as well as to a cross section of the economy-class passengers. People say I can't waste the time – but it's not a waste. It is real market research. I make the time to reply, by getting up early in the mornings. If they have a complaint, I make sure that the problem is resolved.

This market research of mine is important, because we don't always get it right the first time around and when we get it wrong, I will move heaven and earth to change it. Four or five years ago, Virgin Atlantic introduced a new first-class sleeper seat, but customer feedback revealed that it wasn't quite right. Our customers complained that the seats didn't fully recline, which they expected with a sleeper. Rather than living with it for several years in order to recoup the outfitting investment in the wrong seats, we just decided to start again, even though we would be throwing away £35 million. The replacement seats that did fully recline cost an additional £70 million. There's no room for second best in the airline business.

I will get out there all the time and talk to people. I will, for example, always try to get to the V Festival, a good old-fashioned rock festival that we started in 1996. Ten years ago I would say, 'I think I'll go for a wander to publicise it.' But it's now so popular it sells out in a day, with over 120,000 people coming over the weekend to both venues, Chelmsford in Essex and Staffordshire, and there's no need to keep publicising in the same way – so instead, I go out on my own and stop to chat among the big, friendly crowd to see what they think. The reaction last year was fantastic, with loads of people coming up and saying, thank you so much for doing the festival, it's the highlight of my year.

I have become a firm believer that the chairman and chief exec of companies should go out and promote their businesses. The American phrase, 'put your ass on the line' is valid. It makes me angry sometimes when I see companies in crisis with tens of thousands of employees hiding behind the word 'no comment' and nobody being available. In any organisation the buck has to stop somewhere. And in Virgin we're very lucky to have people who realise that while occasionally for legal reasons one cannot comment, it is always better to put your foot forward in any situation, and that applies to the bad times as well as the good times. We have a philosophy in our organisation of apologising when we screw up, and encouraging all of our managing directors and all of our senior employees – who are empowered to do so – to get out and comment on situations and be engaged in the debate, rather than becoming the subject of a debate that you refuse to enter into.

People get fixated on certain brand names appealing to certain age groups, but I think that's ageist. If a brand expands its ideas and philosophies of how to do business and ways in which you go about doing business – as opposed to products – then the brand can appeal in a much more multi-generational sense. If you're someone in your sixties and buy a Virgin holiday and it makes you feel a bit younger than buying something called a Saga holiday, all well and good. There are lots of brands with multi-generational appeal, but people have never thought of them as brands very much. An example is the BBC, which has come on with leaps and bounds as a brand. From the World Service and the *Today* programme, to Children's TV, to BBC Worldwide web coverage and programmes like *Dr Who*, it has managed to create a ubiquitous worldwide news media and information brand, whose appeal crosses generations, colours, creeds and races around the world. It's very much like our diverse charity programme, Virgin Unite – and I welcome it.

Marketing insiders define a good brand as having sex appeal. This means that the customer falls in love with it, desires it, wants it – and buys into it. Sexy is youthful, trendy, fun, cool, whatever your age. Definitely, sexy is very cool. I want Virgin to be the coolest brand on the planet and for that, I'm prepared to dangle in the buff over Times Square, fly over Everest in a balloon, or find myself on a bunjee 100 feet below a helicopter in a skydiver position, to be landed among 100 buxom and beautiful female lifeguards on Bondi Beach to promote Virgin Blue. It's not all tough.

If you're starting your own company, a good lesson would be to think very hard about your image and how to brand it. You can't do better than listen to Freddie Laker's words: 'get out there and use yourself.' If you're passionate about your product, you'll get other people to believe in it too.

11. BE INNOVATIVE

Nothing is impossible
Think creatively
The system is not sacred
To win you have to break the rules
Play the hand you've been dealt with
Find another way

My earliest lessons in lateral thinking and innovation weren't obvious to me at the time. When I was eight years old, in keeping with our family tradition, I was sent away to boarding school. It was a preparatory school near Windsor and I seemed very far from home. On the first night, in the dormitory, I felt incredibly desolate, lonely and frightened. Perhaps I worked myself up, because suddenly I vomited all over the bedclothes. Matron was sent for and instead of being sympathetic, like my mother would have been, she made me clear it up myself. Worse was to follow. I seemed to be constantly breaking some unwritten rule about which I had no idea and, as a reward, was caned.

That was bad enough, but having to thank the headmaster politely for the privilege of having so much pain inflicted on my posterior was incredible. A bigger problem was that I was dyslexic. Words were just a meaningless jumble to me, and however hard I struggled to read and spell, I couldn't for a long time, until I trained myself to concentrate over several years. Constant caning for failing in class made things worse.

But I could run like the wind, and weave through the rugby pitch like a hare. It dawned on me that if I couldn't shine in class, I could play the hand I'd been dealt with. I threw all my energy into sports and became captain of the football, rugby and cricket teams and won all the cups for sprinting and hurdling. I even broke the school long-jump record. English public schools adored and lauded their sporting heroes. Bullies patted me on the back, the masters suddenly mysteriously ignored my shortcomings in the classroom and all my troubles seemed behind me. I can remember the summer when my parents and my sister, Lindi, sat and clapped energetically in the white marquee as I went up to collect every single cup and was proclaimed Victor Laudorum. Grinning broadly, I felt very proud, perhaps not even realising that I had demonstrated an important lesson in life: find another way to succeed.

Sadly, my newfound glory wasn't to last. The following term, I badly tore the cartilage in my right knee in a football match and was in agony. I was carted off to hospital, then sent home to recuperate. I was lying morosely in bed, when Mum came in and said, 'Just think of Douglas Bader. He hasn't got any legs at all. He's playing golf and flying planes and everything. You don't want to be rolling around in bed doing nothing all day, do you?'

Unable to do sports for a long time until my leg healed, I was again thrown to the wolves when I failed all my tests at school. Dad's solution was to send me to a crammer on the Sussex coast, where I did no better. If anything, this school was worse than the previous one, because I was beaten with ghastly regularity. Instead, my consolation prize was my first sexual experience. I was young, yes, but obviously precocious because the headmaster's luscious eighteen-year-old daughter took to me and allowed me into her bed for nocturnal frolics. At the time she was doing part-time work as the matron in another boys' house. I'd climb out of my dormitory window and creep over to her house to pay her a visit, before returning at dawn to my own cold, hard, bed. One night, I was caught by a master on my way back through my window and the next morning, summonsed to the headmaster's study.

When challenged, I could only tell the truth. 'I was on my way back from your daughter's room, sir.'

I was promptly expelled and my parents were told to come and collect me. I knew they would be upset, so thinking fast, I wrote a suicide note and on the envelope said it wasn't to be opened until the next day. I gave it to a boy I knew was far too nosy not to open it at once. Then I sauntered off at a snail's pace over the playing fields, towards the cliffs. When I heard a crowd of boys and teachers coming in hot pursuit, I slowed down even further until they caught up with me and dragged me, so they thought, back from the brink. The expulsion was overturned and when my parents arrived, instead of the lecture I expected, even though I admitted that I had no intention of committing suicide, they were very nice to me. My father even said the headmaster's daughter was rather pretty!

After that, I tried to work with my dyslexia, by concentrating and developing my memory, which has stood me in good stead. I also believe dyslexia has made me more intuitive, because when presented with a written proposal, I am able to cut through pages of detailed facts and figures, instead extrapolating and expanding creatively on the concept as a whole.

I have never forgotten the lessons I learned at that early age and always pass them on to other people who complain about some 'perceived' hardship in their lives. I tell them, don't let your drawbacks hold you back and use the hand you've been dealt to advantage. Your problems are probably never as bad as you think they are and there's always a way.

I have always believed that nothing is set in stone; the System is not sacred. An example of this is how I came to live on an exotic houseboat in the heart of London. One day, I drove along a new street and suddenly found myself in a place known as Little Venice. It was like going through a secret door and arriving in the countryside. I gazed in delight at a line of gaily painted houseboats which were moored in that tranquil backwater, with pots of red geraniums on their decks. There was rosebay willow herb growing along the banks and ducks swimming. I missed the country where I had grown up, and had always loved messing about with boats during our idyllic family holidays at the seaside. This is where I wanted to live. I drove round to the local council offices to ask how I could acquire a houseboat. The officials there sighed and shook their heads. 'Oh well, you have to ask the Water Board, but there's a long waiting list. You might get one in about five years, if you apply now,' they said dolefully.

I didn't bother to apply and returned to the canal, deciding that there must be a way round the system. As I drove along the street, my car died, something it often did. I got out and stood contemplating it, and as I did so, I heard someone call out with an Irish accent. 'Do you want a hand with that?' It was an old man, fixing a stovepipe chimney on the roof of a houseboat.

I walked across the road towards him and told him what I really wanted was to live on one of these boats. 'How should I go about finding one?' I asked.

He smiled. I have just sold one of my boats to a young woman – he waved along the canal – 'There are two bedrooms, and she might be looking for a lodger.'

It turned out he was right; she did want a lodger. Her name was Mundy and her friendly Labrador was called Friday. Mundy and I fell for each other within twenty minutes of meeting and it became my joke that I had the week pretty well sewn up between Mundy and Friday. Later, she found someone else and I ended up buying the houseboat from her. Forty years later, I still have a houseboat moored in Little Venice. If I hadn't been innovative and looked for another way, instead of blindly accepting what the red-tape brigade in the council offices had told me, I would never have found such a great place to live.

I remember once when I had to fight red tape in the shape of a blackmailing neighbour. It was shortly after I had bought our lovely old manor house near Oxford, to use as a recording studio. We had planning permission to record during the day, but most musicians preferred to work at night and sleep during the day, so we applied for planning permission to record at night. The Manor was miles from other houses but we discovered that a certain neighbour, who complained that we kept him awake at night, was the only person blocking our application. When we found that he used to prowl up our drive at night time to check upon us, we engaged in a bit of clandestine warfare and devised a Heath Robinson warning system. One of us – usually me – would hide in the ditch at the bottom of the drive among the stinging nettles and cowslips, with a long piece of string attached to tin cans in the studio. As soon as this man came into view, I would yank the string, the tin cans would descend with a loud clatter onto the heads of the musicians and they'd rush for the kitchen, where they'd sit about drinking coffee. Sometimes a police car would turn up and we just had time to jangle the early warning system. After a few false starts, the police gave up answering our annoying neighbour's callouts.

When Paul and Linda McCartney came to record *Band on the Run* one hot June, Linda kept flinging open the studio door for fresh air. Someone would then close it and Linda would open it again, and music would flood out over the fragrant summer night. Obviously, we couldn't carry on like that and I was at my wits' end, until one day, an elderly couple arrived on the doorstep and asked if we were having trouble with our neighbour. I admitted we were, and they told me our difficult neighbour had blocked their planning application to convert their barn into a home until they paid him off. 'He's after a backhander. Someone should stop him,' they said.

The next day, I bought a small tape recorder and a microphone, stuck it inside my shirt and went around to have a chat with the troublemaker. Sure enough, the question of money came up. He said he'd spent a lot on lawyers blocking our application and asked for a huge sum. I got it all down on tape, sent him a copy and heard no more. My advice to people is to never take defeat lying down. Sometimes, you have to think laterally and be creative to win.

A modest but important example of being hands on and innovative was our Liverpool record shop, which we opened in the spring of 1972. I have mentioned how we filled our shops with cushions and made them nice places to hang out in, but sometimes they were too comfortable. Our first week's takings in Liverpool were excellent, but soon they started to slip on a downhill spiral. I went to Liverpool to see what was happening. When I walked in, the shop was packed, the lights were dim and there was a haze of pot and incense floating overhead. Mods were in one corner, rockers in another and hippies were draped all over the cushions near the till. It was like a nightclub, where non-members couldn't get in, far less reach the till. I installed brighter lights, moved the till closer to the door, and put somebody on the door for a month to warn people gently as they entered that it wasn't a nightclub. Takings recovered and the shop returned to being profitable.

From this, I learned that we should always check on apparent anomalies in person. Once the problem is identified, we can quickly nip the problem in the bud by looking at lateral ways to resolve it.

After some years running Virgin Music, and then having started Virgin Atlantic, I was no stranger to healthy competition. However, there's a big difference between healthy competition and dirty tricks. When we first set up the airline our maintenance was carried out by British Caledonian. When British Airways (BA) took over B-Cal, they promised the Department of Transport and the Civil Aviation Authority (CAA) that they would honour all existing maintenance contracts. But they obviously intended going about it in a less than friendly way. First BA's engineers made some glaring errors when they failed to spot damage to a pylon, the link between the engine and the wing. Inspection showed it up, and a new pylon was ordered, by which time we had lost our space in the hangar. Then, when the pylon arrived, incredibly, they welded the struts upside down. Altogether, the delay cost us sixteen days at the busiest flying season.

When I telephoned the Chief Executive of BA to complain, telling him, 'Your engineering was so bad it could have brought an aircraft down,' his offhand reply was, 'That's one of the perils of being in the aviation business. If you'd stuck to popular music you wouldn't have had this problem.'

In addition, our average charge for labour for servicing our planes went up from £16 to £61 an hour. Obviously, this looked like a typing mistake, and I thought it was – but it wasn't. It was so transparent, my blood boiled. Since BA was the only company with hangar space wide enough to service 747s, they thought they had us over a barrel. Instead, we chose to fly our planes to Ireland to be serviced by Aer Lingus, even though it was expensive and inconvenient. Once again, I had learned never to give in to bullying or to accept things at face value, but to find another way.

To stop monopoly, we had been awarded B-Cal's four flights to Tokyo from Gatwick, but to be viable, we needed to fly daily, from Heathrow. The Japanese government created two extra frequencies – four slots – to Tokyo and we asked for them. BA assumed they were entitled to them; but historically, we won them. Lord King at BA was furious and claimed that by allowing us those slots, BA would lose £250 million a year. 'That is £250 million of revenue lost to our public shareholders which has gone straight into Richard Branson's back pocket,' he seethed, which was untrue and unfair.

We were delighted by the breakthrough and I got the team together to crack open some bottles of champagne. We had celebrated prematurely; BA owned all the available check-in desks at Heathrow and baggage handling facilities, and they wouldn't let us use them because they said they were running to capacity. My parents had always drilled into me their motto, 'Nothing ventured, nothing gained', and I decided I wasn't going to roll over and die. Instead, I decided to stroll around Terminal 3 at Heathrow Airport myself and do a little investigating. I saw a whole line of empty check-in desks and asked, 'Whose are those?'

'British Airways,' I was told. I made a note of it and got the use of them.

Then, when I asked for more slots to fly to New York, we were palmed off with flights at ridiculous hours or, with some, we could fly out but not return. In the end, it was only the threat of filing a lawsuit at the European Court that won me the facilities and all the slots I wanted at Heathrow. It wasn't as if I were stealing all this; legally it was available under the rules of fair competition. But it was only by being persistent and innovative that we won the day.

We got some revenge on BA by using their own promotion against them. On 10 June 1986, BA ran a promotion to give away 5,200 seats for travel from New York to London. Immediately, we ran an advertisement that said, 'It has always been Virgin's policy to encourage you to fly to London for as little as possible. So on June 10 we encourage you to fly British Airways.' The British Airways promotion generated a lot of interest, but most of the news coverage included a mention of our cheeky advertisement. British Airways paid a lot for their promotion – but we reaped a large slice of publicity at a very low cost.

Some years later when the London Eye – a great landmark sponsored by BA for the Millennium celebrations – was in the difficult process of being erected on the South Bank of the River Thames, opposite the Houses of Parliament, the engineers failed on their first attempt. It so happens that I own an airship company. Now, I'm not admitting to anything, but it wasn't long before an airship, painted red in Virgin's colours, was seen floating above the London Eye, proclaiming, 'BA can't get it up.' It is things like this that put the fun into business.

We did well because we never stopped putting our customers first, and tried to give them what they wanted, regardless of the cost. A lot of executives consistently do what's easiest or cheapest for the business rather than the people paying the freight. I always tell people, 'Take a look at your business and ask yourself, "Is this how I would want to be treated if I were the customer?"' I never stop looking for innovative ways to do this. One time, flying across the Atlantic, I wanted to talk to the pretty girl in the next aisle, but I was stuck in my seat the entire flight, which was boring. This inspired me to introduce stand-up bars in Virgin's cabins, and feedback tells us that this is now one of our main selling points. When my wife Joan's manicurist suggested offering nail treatments and massages on Virgin's flights, I didn't even bother with market research. I immediately thought it sounded like a great idea and said, 'Screw it, let's do it.' Now we have 700 nail and massage therapists on staff.

Singapore Airlines became our partners in Virgin Atlantic, paying a record £600 million for a 49 per cent stake in the company. In 2000 I started a new airline in Australia called Virgin Blue. It did very well, doubling passengers and driving prices down. Our success culminated with a buy-out offer from Air New Zealand, who was the parent company to Ansett, Virgin Blue's main rival in Australia. The offer was $250 million; but there was a slight twist to this because Singapore Airlines, our partners in Virgin Atlantic, had a 20 per cent stake in ANZ. The CEO of Singapore Airlines telephoned, with the encouraging words: 'Richard, I really think you should accept this offer. It's a very generous valuation and if you don't take it, we'll put the money and more into Ansett instead and they will wipe out Virgin Blue within six months.'

The offer wasn't a bad one, though I thought undervalued, but there was something about his voice on the long-distance line that told me he could be bluffing. I decided to play my hand. I called a press conference, mainly to illustrate to the competition authorities how strongly the public felt about the need for competition, which led to cheap tickets. Keeping a straight face, I stood before the gathered press and looking suitably sombre, I announced, 'This is a sad day, but I've decided to sell up. This means that cheap air tickets in Australia will be a thing of the past. Our staff will be part of Ansett and there will be redundancies. But anyway, I've done well out of it, so I'm off back to the UK right away with my $250 million profit.' I waved the cheque in the air.

There was a stunned silence. Mouths fell open in shock, until a journalist from the Press Association gathered her wits and rushed off to be the first to file her copy. She should have hung around for a few moments longer. As I glanced across the room, for the first time I noticed some of Virgin Blue's staff, who weren't supposed to be there. They were in tears. 'Only joking,' I said hastily, and in front of everyone tore up the cheque.

My stunt had the desired result of giving my reply to ANZ. Five days later, Ansett went bust. Singapore Airlines never gave them the money and Virgin Blue suddenly became Australia's second largest carrier.

My sense of humour didn't abandon me when in 2003 I asked to be allowed to operate flights from London to Sydney on what is rather disparagingly known as the 'Kangaroo Route'. When I heard that Geoff Dixon of Qantas had been making some demeaning remarks about Virgin, I wrote him an open letter:

Dear Geoff,

I was amused to read Qantas's completely dismissive comments about Virgin Atlantic's chances of getting permission to fly to Australia. It would be prudent for you to remind yourself of your and James Strong's equally dismissive comments about Virgin Blue's chances of entering the Australian market only three years ago.

Here goes! This is the gist of what you said:

'Virgin Blue is a lot of media hype.'

'This market is not big enough to sustain Virgin Blue.'

'Virgin Blue doesn't have deep enough pockets to cope.'

'Qantas will employ any option to see off this interloper.'

'They'll be unlikely to survive a year.'

'Claims by Richard Branson that domestic fares are high are a misnomer!' (my exclamation mark)

Here is what James Strong, your former CEO, said about Virgin Blue and myself:

'If you listen to most of the pretenders there is a distinct air that they are making it up as they go along. In terms of real plans and real commitment you could fire a shot gun up the main street and not hit anybody.'

Yet three years later you are telling your staff that this same airline, 'that was making it up as it went along' and that now has 30 per cent of the market could, 'Drive Qantas out of business!' We also find it flattering, if a little silly, that three years on you now have spies hiding behind pot plants in the Virgin terminal trying to work out why we are so successful.

Even if some of your comments don't suggest it, your actions indicate you are taking us seriously. But let's not take ourselves too seriously. I would like to propose a friendly challenge!

If Virgin Atlantic fails to fly to Australia (within 18 months, say) I'd be prepared to suffer the indignity of donning one of your stewardesses brand new designer outfits and will work your flight from London to Australia serving your customers throughout.

However, if Virgin Atlantic does fly to Australia you would do so instead. On our inaugural flight from London to Australia you would wear one of our beautiful red Virgin Stewardesses uniforms and serve our inaugural guests all the way to Australia. Oh and in case you were wondering, we're not hung up on flying through Hong Kong. You might end up doing your day's work experience through Singapore, Thailand or Malaysia instead.

This is the challenge. If you believe in what Qantas said to the press there can't be any risk for you. We expect your response within one week. Our inaugural flights are great fun and I look forward to welcoming you on

board personally. Oh and by the way my
preferred drink is . . .!
Kind regards,
Richard.
p.s. I enclose a picture to give you an idea of
what you might look like.

The photograph showed a mock up of Geoff Dixon's
head atop a shapely stewardess posing in Virgin's
stylish red uniform. Needless to say, CEO Dixon's
response was not polite. I don't know what his
private comments were when we operated the route
twelve months later.

Obviously, not everyone reading this will have to
deal with the huge financial risks and the skulldug-
gery involved in launching a new airline; but the
principles are the same whatever your challenge is:
don't give up, stick to your guns and find another
way.

Efficiency is fine, but things move so fast in the
modern world that it's better to be innovative, fresh
and original than lose the spark over routine or
nitpicking ways. The world is changing. Ideas and
opportunities are expanding fast. Sometimes, your
ideas don't take off. Even after careful research, not
all ideas are good; sometimes your competitors have
better ideas or they're there faster than you. The
modern entrepreneur takes failure in his or her stride
and moves on. You can learn from ideas that haven't
worked and use it to know when to play the hand or
when to fold. A simple example is when our retail
team decided to sell orchids instead of red roses on
Valentine's Day, 1988. There was either not enough

promotion or customers just didn't want them – but we sold only 50 out of 50,000 and were left with piles of wilting and dying flowers. I hate waste, and to me this was an indication of a deeper problem within Retail. We reorganised and never again had to throw away tons of anything.

If starting an airline from scratch with no prior experience was the most innovative thing I've done, then moving into trains was the second. Equally, it also took many people by surprise. I was never a trainspotter and didn't have a toy train set. In our family, activities were more the thing. We were fortunate to live in the country and could make our own fun. I am one of the few people who has come into the train business from the outside who wasn't a train fanatic. People have said when we did get into trains, we moved really fast. Our decision was fast, but setting things up took a long time, so 'fast' is a matter of degree. When you're changing infrastructure, change is something that can take several years. To make the omelette you have to crack the eggs. Virgin setting up the West Coast Mainline and the story of rail privatisation was like making an omelette.

The railways in the UK had been nationalised by the Attlee Labour government in 1947 and had gone into a steady decline. In the UK, British Rail was a nationalised industry, fraught with union problems and a massive lack of investment in the infrastructure and rolling stock; consequently, it seemed to make sense to the Conservatives, first under Margaret Thatcher and followed through by John Major, to reprivatise in 1996 and get in fresh money and energy. To start with, rail privatisation was very confusing; but at the end of the day it works as well as can be expected, given the fact that it has been operating for a relatively short period after years of starvation. Now at least we have a more modern fleet of trains in Britain, railway lines, infrastructure and services are back on a more regular pathway and the expenditure has been made that had been neglected for forty years. The Railway was a declining business because the state did not invest in it. What rail privatisation brought about was a wave of investment – but it was very badly done.

Looking back, I believe that the Conservatives should not have split up the track and the trains in 1992. Virgin was asked its opinion and we advised, 'Keep the service unified. The same people who operate trains should operate the tracks.' This is how it was developed when railways were first established in the Victorian era. But they were split up in 1992 and it was a disaster because there was no co-ordination or communication between the two sectors – stock and infrastructure. Stock and infrastructure are an integrated unit and if, for example, lines are taken up for repair, train providers need to be told and given a schedule. More often than not, this wasn't done and not only did the public complain constantly, but undone work and bad management often led to major accidents.

The British aviation industry was also broken up and denationalised the following year and again, there were problems. These weren't as obvious as in the railways, but nevertheless, there are limits to how effective such a split has proved to be. The airline industry can't work holistically in terms of reducing carbon emissions, for example. With global warming a real issue, it is now up to us to make the linkages to allow the airport authority to work in tandem with the airlines and air traffic authority to reduce emissions and the amount of fuel used. I have suggested that one way fuel and carbon emissions might be cut is to tow planes to starting grids on the runway, so they don't run their engines – often for very long periods – until ten minutes before takeoff. I believe that this simple step would reduce carbon emissions by more than fifty per cent at Heathrow and nearly ninety per cent at JFK. It would also mean that planes flying across the Atlantic would carry two tons less fuel in the air, which would reduce CO_2 even further. Fuel-efficient new planes would be another step. These efforts alone would reduce the world's aviation emissions by up to twenty-five per cent.

When it comes to the rail industry, the train operators have ended up coming through and most of them have succeeded in improving the service compared to what it was like before – and in some cases quite dramatically. The growth in the number of people who now travel by rail in Britain is the fastest anywhere in the world. Passenger numbers on Virgin West Coast have gone up from 13.6 million in 1997/8 to 18.7 million in 2005/6; while passenger numbers on Virgin Cross Country have almost doubled in the same period, from 12.6 million to 20.4 million. Travelling times have also been reduced. All this has been achieved with an infrastructure half the size of that in 1946.

But the biggest innovation of all is Virgin Trains' radical new approach to the environment, one we are totally committed to. The drive now is to reduce carbon emissions by trying to get even more people back into trains and off the roads. There have been various suggestions as to how this should happen, including restoring tracks to the pre-Beeching levels, widening tracks, or having two-tier trains. Where two-tier trains are concerned, you have to think of the cost relative to the benefit of heightening thousands of tunnels and the time it would take to do so. Instead of widening tracks, it would be better to make longer platforms and longer trains. I'd rather invest in putting more track back on the existing railway lines and improving the infrastructure than building altogether new railway lines – with the exception of ones like the Eurostar lines being built into London at the moment. A far better investment case was getting the West Coast Mainline running. These core railway lines have to work very well to compete with airlines to get people back into trains or to compete with cars on the motorway. Two-track railway is the equivalent of roundabouts on motorways.

High-speed Maglev trains have been suggested as an ecologically friendly solution, but the truth is, Britain is a small island, with lots of towns and cities and short lengths of track between them. We don't have the vast distances of countries like France, Russia, the USA, Canada and Australia; while Japan, although being an island like Britain, is a very long country. The idea of rebuilding the whole of Britain for Maglev trains with speeds of 300 mph is a fantasy. Quite simply, they wouldn't be able to stop and start in the short spaces between stations. The investment–energy ratio just doesn't work. The trains themselves are incredibly heavy in terms of their electricity usage. By the time you've used all that energy to make an entirely new infrastructure, the payback would be a hundred years and twice the amount of CO_2 pumped into the atmosphere.

The most important thing we need to concentrate on in businesses like transport is to look at the infrastructure that exists. What do you need to replace it with? What is the cost–emission ratio? When we built the Pendolino (tilting) trains for the West Coast Mainline we thought through three things. Weight: we built these trains very light, out of aluminium, not steel, and we're the first fleet in Britain to be built out of aluminium. Energy expended in braking: we put regenerative braking in them, as in the Toyoto Prius cars. Fuel: we built an electromagnetic as opposed to a hydraulic turbo system, which is very simple and light and uses much less equipment. We want a system that will be energy-efficient and which will run for a very long time. These are more important to us than the 'cost' in economic terms, which led to us building relatively expensive trains for the West Coast Mainline – but they are the most electricity efficient trains in the whole of Western Europe, for long-distance trains. They came into service in 2003–04 and if you compare them with the old trains, for instance, that run on the East Coast Mainline, or the very big diesel trains that First Great Western still run on the Great Western line, the CO_2 impact is less than half those trains. It is nine times more efficient to travel as a passenger from London to Glasgow on a Pendolino than it is to go in a 737 aeroplane, assuming both are full, which is a fair comparison

This is part of Virgin's Gaia Capitalism approach to business and enterprise in the twenty-first century and beyond. I'm convinced that it's the way of the future and vital to the health of our planet, even if it costs more in terms of economic profit. We will profit, but in an entirely different and more crucial way. However, we have to do it properly because there's no point in operating at a loss because we'd just go bust and someone else who might not be as environmentally aware as we are would just step in and fill the gap. (I expanded on Gaia Capitalism and the environment in Chapter 9.)

I firmly believe that if we are to save the world from the biggest disaster to befall the human race we have to go into innovative overdrive. It doesn't mean we have to stop living normally. We don't have to return to travelling by foot, donkey or camel and buying our food, clothing and shoes from local farmers' markets (though there's nothing wrong with that); but we do have to work hard at developing a way of reducing, then ultimately bringing down, CO_2 emissions to safe levels. It's not beyond us to work out how to live happy and full lives without doing harm to the world.

The lesson I have learned is that an innovative approach can open up to some fascinating new opportunities. It could lead to a renaissance in invention and science.

12. DO SOME GOOD

Change the world, even if in a small way
Make a difference and help others
Do no harm
Always think what you can do to help

I was brought up to think we could all change the world. I believed that it was our duty to help others and to do good when we could; but it was never onerous. It was more a matter of being helpful to family, friends and neighbours in the village and getting a buzz from a job well done. When I went to boarding school I still managed to come up with creative and (I thought) useful ideas. I'm sure my headmaster was stunned when I wrote a long report about how he could run the school better. I ended grandly with the words, 'I would be very interested in your views on this, and any money saved could be put towards my next plan . . .'

He didn't laugh, or even cane me for my cheek. He handed back my report and said dryly, 'Very good, Branson. Put it in the school magazine.'

Instead, I left school and started my own magazine, seeing it as a platform to change things.

When my sister Lindi and I were trying to sell copies of *Student* in the street, a tramp asked me for money. I didn't have a penny, but I was so fired up to do good, I tore off my clothes and gave them to him. I had to borrow a blanket before I was arrested. Gandhi may have walked across India wrapped in a sheet to make a point, but shuffling along in an old blanket somehow didn't have the same cachet.

One of the ways we tried to help people our age was by starting the Student Advisory Centre, somewhere anonymous and friendly, staffed by student volunteers who were on the same wavelength and understood the problems. People could ask about anything, from flats to grants, but mostly they asked for advice about sex. Oddly, I have a family connection, albeit a tenuous one, to Marie Stopes, the original doyen of women's health and sexual education, dating back from when Mum, at the age of twelve, had appeared in a West End revue written by Mrs Stopes. However, my inspiration was born out of need, when one of my girlfriends needed an abortion. At the time, there was nowhere else to go for the kind of advice we offered, free of charge at all hours. Gradually, the centre took more and more of my time. I would be talking to someone suicidal at three in the morning, advising pregnant girls as to who was the nicest doctor they could go to see and telling someone else about the hours the venereal disease clinic was open at Charing Cross Hospital. In the little time left, I would try to run the magazine. When we started the centre, in the crypt of an historic old church in central London, it was manned by volunteers who handed out phone numbers, details and contacts that helped point people in the right direction to seek help for a whole range of pressing issues. It did so well that, 35 years later, it's still going strong, though under a new name.

The magazine eventually went, to be replaced by the record company and then the airline, then all the other companies. I spent the next few years building up Virgin. Making money was in order to survive and pay the bills, but my aim was to be creative and have fun. My creativity became chan-nelled into business because, for example, while originally I just wanted to write and edit a magazine, I needed to learn fast how to be a publisher to make it pay. I also happen to find hard work challenging. The man who started IKEA divides his day into ten-minute sections. He says, 'Ten minutes, once gone, are gone for good. Divide your life into ten-minute units, and don't waste even a minute.'

You don't have to fill your time rushing about in order to use your time wisely, though. Bill Gates – the world's top charity donor – said his staff at Microsoft could spend two hours gazing into space, as long as their minds were working, and Albert Einstein came up with the theory of relativity in his head without paper or pen. He only wrote it down later. To be honest, I work out all my best ideas in my head too – but then write them down! And because I don't use my hands for my work, perhaps that is why I enjoy taking time off for hard physical tasks, like crossing the Atlantic in a boat, going camping with my dad in the bush, ballooning, or being hands on with some of the entrepreneurial enterprises I've helped found for young people in Africa.

It's said that love of money is the root of all evil. It doesn't have to be. Money can be used for good. The biggest charities in the world were started by rich men and women, but some were begun with next to nothing. Harvard, the wealthiest college in America, is a charitable trust. It started with a few books and just $350. IKEA started in a garden shed. Its parent company is a charitable trust. The man who dreamed up the Big Mac started life selling paper cups. He was someone else who didn't believe in wasting time. 'If you have time to lean, you have time to clean,' he always told his staff. Perhaps he was not in a hurry because he didn't get the idea for McDonald's until he was aged 52. His company now gives $50 million a year to charity.

So money can be a force for good. But you don't need to be rich to do good. Children used to collect silver paper and empty cola tins to raise money for good causes. Today, they go on charity runs or donate to Live Aid. My son Sam and I are going to do an Arctic crossing to raise awareness for global warming. There are many ways of helping others. One very simple way is to do no harm and that costs nothing at all.

When I turned forty, I was at an all-time low. We were battling with British Airways for space in the skies. We had been voted Best Business Class Airline of the year, but it was a constant fight to find enough money to keep going. It was only Virgin Music's string of hit records that was keeping us afloat. Simon, who ran Virgin Music, seemed to be losing interest in it – mostly because he thought the airline would bankrupt us. I sat down and looked back at my life. I asked myself if I should do something new, if I should have a complete change. I had never been a big reader, but I had started to read some quite solid biographies and to my surprise had found them very absorbing. My life was so hectic, the idea of having more time to read was quite appealing.

One day, I said to Joan, 'I think I might go to college and do a degree in history.'

'You just want to chase pretty girls,' was her blunt reply.

Was she right? Was I facing a midlife crisis? Perhaps. So, instead of thinking what I could do for myself, I wondered if I could do more for others. I thought I might look into politics. I could use my business skills to do some good on major issues, such as fighting cigarette companies. I could fund a cure for cancer, look into health care, or help homeless people. There were many things I could do that would make me feel useful. I have gone on to follow this path in the rest of my life.

I believe we should all assess our lives from time to time. Have we reached our goals? Are there things we can weed out that we don't need? I'm not talking about throwing away old shoes or broken chairs. I mean we need to lose our bad habits or lazy ways that hold us back and clutter our minds.

My cousin, Sir Peter Scott, ran a famous wetlands bird reserve at Slimbridge in Gloucestershire. When I told him I wanted a lake at my home in Oxford to attract wild birds, he came and gave me advice. I dug out a lake and built several islands for birds to nest on. Swans, ducks, geese and herons flew in from all over the place. It's a very peaceful spot, somewhere I can think things through. Normally I like to be in a crowd of people or with my family, but sometimes you need space. I like to walk around the lake on my own, just thinking.

I think we all need some kind of retreat or place of our own. On a literary level, the novelist Virginia Woolf defined it as 'a room of one's own' but it doesn't have to be an actual room. It has to be a space to think without interruption, even if it's in one's head.

When I was fighting to survive with the airline, it was one of the few times when I felt totally lost. As I walked around the lake I had some big decisions to make. When I had told the bank that Virgin Music was worth at least a billion dollars, they had wanted me to sell the company to cover their loans to the airline. I had two choices: to close the airline or sell the record company. The problem was that I thought I could keep both. I just needed the bank to keep its nerve. It seemed to me that, as long as they knew how valuable the music side was, their debt was safe. But banks don't like risk and they said that if I didn't sell it they would withdraw my loans. I wasn't sure what to do. I loved Virgin Music and knew that as a company it would continue to grow. We had just signed the Rolling Stones and Janet Jackson, and I felt as if I would be letting them and all our other musicians down. I wasn't sure what to do on that rainy day as I walked around the lake, pondering my options.

In the middle of this worrying time, in August 1990, Iraq invaded Kuwait. I heard on the news that 150,000 refugees had crossed into Jordan. I was friends with King Hussein and Queen Noor of Jordan. The queen was a beautiful woman, a highly trained Arab-American architect who had met her husband when she was working for Royal Jordanian Airlines. We had a lot of things in common. Our friendship had started two years earlier in 1998, when she had seen me on TV during my balloon flight around the world and phoned to ask if I would teach the royal family to fly in a balloon.

I had shipped a balloon to Jordan and met the royal family. They were all as lovely as she was and the children were polite and friendly. I had a great time, flying over the capital, looking down on ancient, red-tiled roofs. When the people below realised that their king and queen were floating along in a wicker basket above their heads, they ran along, looking up and cheering. With the Middle East in turmoil, it was a difficult time for the king, who had been educated in England and was a friend of our country. There had been many attempts on his life and armed bodyguards were always around him – but that day, as we floated overhead, the bodyguards were in a dilemma, unable to protect their ruler when he was up in the sky without them. But for King Hussein it was a welcome moment of complete freedom.

When Saddam Hussein invaded Kuwait in 1990, I watched the thousands of refugees flooding over the border on the television and picked up the phone to ask King Hussein and Queen Noor if I could help. I wanted to do something positive and make a difference in some way to the lives of those refugees. The queen said she would see what needed to be done and would get back to me. Later that day she phoned to ask if I could get them some blankets. She said the desert was very hot during the day and very cold at night and blankets could be rigged up to give shade during the day and at night people could roll up in them to keep warm.

'A few very young children have already died,' Queen Noor said.

'How many blankets do you need?' I asked.

She said they needed 100,000. 'But we've got only two or three days before hundreds of people start to die. It's urgent, Richard.'

Virgin airline staff got to work, phoning around. In two days one of our jumbo jets was on its way to Jordan with 40,000 blankets, tons of rice and medical supplies. We returned with British people who had been stranded in Jordan. As soon as I returned to Britain, I was told that the head of British Airways was hopping mad. He said that as the senior airline in Britain, they should have been asked to help first. It was pointed out to him that I had offered and he hadn't. In fact, he had apparently refused to let BA help in international crises, even when approached by Christian Aid. So, at once, he found a load of blankets and rushed them to Jordan. I was pleased that our example had partly pushed him into helping.

When I heard that our supplies had not reached all the refugees, I flew to Jordan and again stayed with the king and queen in the royal palace. I argued with a minister who I knew had blocked things from moving and got him to send the supplies to the refugee camps. I also had long talks with King Hussein about Saddam. The king wanted Jordan to remain neutral in the conflict that by then seemed likely. His country was in a very weak position and he also saw both sides of the picture. He hoped things could be sorted out through talks – but he was worried that the West might go to war to protect the oilfields in Kuwait. He knew there was very little time.

A few days later I was watching the news in London, when I saw Saddam on the TV. He had taken British hostages and was using them as a human shield. I thought about what I could do to help. I was one of the very few Western people who had direct access to King Hussein. He in turn was one of the very few people that Saddam trusted. We could cut out all the angry people in the middle and perhaps get somewhere before there was a war. I felt that Saddam could exchange the hostages for medical supplies and that perhaps King Hussein could talk to Saddam and put my suggestion to him. I called Queen Noor and asked if she could help with my plan.

'Come on out and stay with us, Richard. You can discuss it with the king yourself,' she said.

In Jordan yet again, I spent three days talking to King Hussein. He agreed that something must be done quickly before things got worse. I sat down and with a lot of care wrote a very polite letter by hand to Saddam. I asked if he would release all the foreigners who were trapped in Iraq. To show goodwill I would fly in medical supplies that Iraq was short of. I signed it, 'Yours respectfully, Richard Branson.'

After dinner that night, the king took my letter to his study and translated it into Arabic. He also wrote his own personal cover letter to Saddam and sent it by special courier to Iraq. I could do no more and flew home.

Two nights later, I heard from King Hussein. It was very good news. Saddam said that he would release the sick hostages and the women and children, but he wanted someone of stature to fly to Iraq and ask him in person, on TV. I phoned Sir Edward Heath, the former prime minister. We got on well because of our mutual interest in boats. Bravely, he agreed to go at once. The plan was that Edward Heath would first fly to Jordan to stay with the royal family. From there, he would get safe passage to Iraq.

A day later, King Hussein phoned me and with his usual quiet courtesy said, 'I have good news for you, sir. You can set off for Iraq. I have Saddam's word that you will be safe.'

I felt I needed to go in person because I was sending our own pilots and crew in the plane, all of whom had volunteered. I had one major worry before we set off. In spite of King Hussein's promise, many expected Saddam to take me and Edward Heath hostage and impound the plane. Because of the risk, we had no insurance. If Saddam did seize the plane, we would go bust. I was risking everything on this venture – but too many people depended on me. There was no backing out.

When we left Iraq with the hostages, the crew and Edward Heath safely on board, we were so relieved we partied all the way back. But one person wasn't happy. The boss of BA said, 'Who the hell does Richard Branson think he is – part of the bloody Foreign Office?'

Afterwards, I wrote in my diary, 'What are the motives for doing such things? A month ago, I was at an all-time low. I seemed to have run out of a purpose in my life. I'd proved myself in many areas. I'd just turned forty. I was seeking a new challenge . . .'

When I re-read what I had written, I realised that as a *businessman* I could do a great deal of good. The rescue mission to Iraq had proved it. As a businessman, I meet incredible people like Nelson Mandela, world leaders like the Russian premier, Vladimir Putin, and people of vast wealth like Bill Gates and Microsoft's lesser-known co-founder Paul Allen. In fact, people in business and the very wealthy are in a unique position. They can connect with everyone, whether high or low, in any country, through a network of good will. One advantage of being a businessman, unlike a politician, is stability. Since I went into business at fifteen, I have seen many different prime ministers. So businessmen have that sense of continuity that politicians don't have.

I believe they can use that power wisely, for the good of the world – exactly as I said in my first ever *Student* column.

I also want to continue to cut through red tape, exactly as I did during the days leading up to the first Gulf War, when we dropped everything and flew out with aid. For example, during the recent tsunami disaster in Sri Lanka, we quickly arranged dedicated aid flights in cooperation with Oxfam. We're fortunate to have three airlines around the world and have set aside a small team of people who can move quickly so that when there are crisis situations in the world, we can react quickly. We managed to get the first flight to Sri Lanka after the tsunami struck, as well as flights into the Maldives and India. Sending water by air is not cost-effective, but when you have desperate people, the cost doesn't come into it. For instance, in Sri Lanka they desperately needed fresh water, so we filled a Boeing 747 with bottled water and just sent it. Oxfam and the other relief agencies know that, whatever the financial cost to us, our planes are available when they need them. And we were also a little cheeky with our regular passenger services. The staff asked for donations for the tsunami – and people were very generous.

My original love, music, is also a strong force for good. You only have to look at Live Aid and Live 8 and the incredible work that people like Peter Gabriel, Bono and Bob Geldof do in raising money for famine relief and other disasters in the Third World to see that. Princess Diana did much for charity when she was alive, and I was pleased to be able to help her with that in some small way. I was proud when I persuaded Elton John to sing 'Candle in the Wind' at her funeral. Persuading the royal family to let him do it was far more challenging. I also got Elton's lyricist, Bernie Taupin, to rewrite the lyrics to 'Candle in the Wind'. The original, written as a tribute to Marilyn Monroe, contained the lyrics, 'the press still hounded you', which obviously wouldn't do.

In 2004 I brought myself closer to my vision of helping more people by setting up Virgin Unite. It is intended as a way of getting all the Virgin staff around the world to work together to help with tough social problems, and I appointed the wonderful Jean Oelwang to run it – she really is an exceptional person. A significant portion of my time is spent on the environment and driving change as well as being hands on, when time allows me, with charities to help the disadvantaged. Obviously, some parts of the world are more disadvantaged than others, and while we do have several projects in the UK and elsewhere in the world, most of our work is in South Africa where I hope we can continue to make a difference.

We have come full circle from where I started out in the world at the Student Advisory Service. It has been renamed the Help Counselling Centre, because the services it provides have been extended to cover a wider range of issues; but it is still free. My daughter Holly, who is in her final year as a medical student, recognises the sexual issues facing young people in the UK, and volunteers when she can at Virgin Unite.

One of the biggest lessons I have learned is that if we set our children an example, they will continue to follow it. It's the only way forward if the people of the world are to help each other.

13. POW! SHAZAM!

Speed is the ultimate competitive weapon
Be first in the field
Do it now
Keep it simple
Cut red tape
Keep your eye on the ball

In today's highly competitive world, the pace of development is picking up. The window of opportunity can be gone in the blink of an eye. If you get a good idea, grab it and develop it fast. Be careful, but not slow. Don't get bogged down in bureaucracy, or overwhelm yourself with red tape or too many cumbersome parameters. Just because you have 'always done it like this' doesn't mean you shouldn't change and adapt. These are the lessons I have learned during my forty years of being a creative entrepreneur.

Many people think that Virgin moves fast; and often we can and do – but you have to be prepared to be called a raving lunatic, as when we launched

Virgin Atlantic with just one plane to our name. From concept to flying took us just three exhausting, delirious months. I don't think Superman could have moved faster. None of us slept for weeks; every day brought new challenges – but we did it.

However, one important lesson I have learned is to think long term: thinking of an idea and waiting for the technology to come around at the right time to achieve the goal. This is what happened when I decided to get into what I call space tourism. Like many innovative ideas, it started out in an almost casual way. But the secret of many groundbreaking advances is to see the angle no matter how small it might seem at first.

My enthusiasm for aviation came out of a number of places. Obviously, there was a bit of family influence, my mother having been one of the first women in the world to be an air hostess, and Second World War ace fighter pilot Douglas Bader being a close friend. I was also indignant by what had happened to Sir Freddie Laker. I thought he had been very badly treated, and when he was put out of business in 1982 and Virgin Atlantic was awarded SkyTrain's licence – the very same one that Freddie had been using – it was as if I'd been handed the baton.

I also love balloons and once I flew in the stratosphere I knew what it was to be fascinated by space. Not only did I follow the exciting adventures of Dan Dare: Pilot of the Future in the *Eagle* comics I was allowed to read as a child (perhaps because they had quite a lot of educational story strips in them) but, more importantly, I was one of those teenagers in the 1960s who watched the moon landing with my parents. It was exciting and I always believed that some day I would get the chance to fly into space. That dream for millions was largely destroyed in 1985 when the world's first real space tourist, Christa McAuliffe, an American schoolteacher, was tragically killed when the Challenger space shuttle exploded. In one fell swoop the dream of the ordinary person to go into space was over.

By the mid-1990s, as a result of the balloon trips around the world, I was becoming increasingly interested in aviation's impact on the environment and I remember sitting in Morocco, waiting for the weather to improve in order to attempt to fly a balloon around the world, and getting into conversation with Buzz Aldrin, Per Lindstrand and Will Whitehorn about why space rockets were launched on the ground, wasting so much fuel and using so much energy to get people or payload into space.

It was actually Buzz Aldrin who said that had not always been the case and when Will asked whether or not a balloon could launch a rocket, Buzz explained that the US military had actually experimented in this field in the early 1950s. He then went on to explain that when the Russians launched Sputnik in 1957 when the space race started the US had a lot of catching up to do. So instead of continuing with experiments of this type, they went for what they considered to be the most logical and easiest expedient of building a massive intercontinental ballistic missile to launch human beings into space. That began a series of programmes that led to the US building larger and larger rockets for manned launchers, and the Russians doing the same thing.

The Americans did have one project during the late 1950s and 1960s, which involved a much more efficient idea of launching an aircraft from great altitude into space, called the X-15 hypersonic project. This remarkable aircraft had an internal structure of titanium and a skin surface of a chrome-nickel alloy known as Inconel X. The first un-powered glide flight took place in 1959, when it was launched from a B-52 aircraft at about 45,000 feet, reaching speeds in excess of 500 mph. By 1963 it had set an altitude record of 354,200 feet (67 miles) and the numerous tests contributed to the development of the Mercury, Gemini, and Apollo piloted space-flight programmes as well as the Space Shuttle programme. But as NASA budgets got squeezed and the Apollo programme became more successful, the X-15 project was abandoned in 1968 after a hundred flights.

That was my first debate about better ways of getting into space. And the next day, I asked Will, who, among his many accomplishments, was an experienced pilot – if the Virgin brand was registered for space travel as a trademark. It turned out that it was, and I asked him to keep a watching brief on the sector to see what technologies came along.

In 1996, Dr Peter Diamandis made waves when he announced the Ansari X-Prize, for the first private manned space flight. He is a Renaissance figure, who had been fascinated by space since childhood. In eighth grade, while living in New York, at about the age of twelve or thirteen, he won first place in the Estes rocket design contest. He went on to graduate from MIT and Harvard Medical School and later became the winner of the Konstantine Tsiolkovsky

Award, the Aviation & Space Technology Laurel, and the 2003 World Technology Award for Space – so when he spoke people listened.

Dr Diamandis came to see us in 1998, to discuss the X-Prize. The prize was ten million dollars for the first people to successfully launch a person into space on a fully reusable space launch system and do it twice in two weeks. It seemed like an impossible dream. To start with, the economics looked hopeless. Every time the Shuttle launched, it cost NASA the best part of a billion dollars – so the idea of designing and building something new, reusable and cost-effective and energy-efficient to make it even worth going after a prize of ten million dollars seemed unachievable. However, the X-Prize sparked a lot of interest and in early 1999, we decided to register the name Virgin Galactic. In addition to that, we began to look at a number of projects that were under way to try and win the X-Prize – but in the end, there was only one contender who gave us the confidence to consider developing his technology. His name is Burt Rutan and he was being funded by Paul Allen, Bill Gates' partner in Microsoft, to enter the competition with a unique technological approach through his company, Scaled Composites. Not only would he launch his rocket from 50,000 feet high, well above the lower atmosphere, but he also planned to build his spaceship out of carbon composite rather than metal, and use a unique hybrid motor that burned laughing gas and rubber.

At the time, we were already working with Burt, who was building the Virgin Atlantic Global Flier, the world's most efficient aircraft, in which adventurer Steve Fossett planned to fly around the world non-stop and unrefuelled in order to get the ultimate records for distance, duration and efficiency of aviation. Alex Tai, one of our Virgin Atlantic captains, was spending a lot of time at Burt's factory on the Global Flyer project, and when they saw the prototype of the SpaceShipOne suborbital, they knew almost instinctively that it was a winner. The beauty of Burt Rutan's design is its simplicity and fuel efficiency.

After SpaceShipOne won the X-Prize, months of hectic negotiation followed and I bought the rights from Paul Allen to build a fleet of spaceships from SpaceShipOne's technology. Virgin Galactic was formally born in September 2006, nearly seven years after the company name was first registered and eleven years after we first looked at the idea in Morocco. It is my intention to take civilian passengers for a ride into space starting in 2008 and, with the exception of Joan – who dislikes flying so much she squeezes my hand when we're flying anywhere – I, my parents and my two children, Holly and Sam, will be the first passengers on the inaugural flight of SpaceShipTwo.

The first market we're looking at for this unique new product is space tourism. But the system itself is about a lot more than simply taking people on the experience of a lifetime. We're going to use space tourism as a means to demonstrate the safety and commercial viability of our new space launch system. It does 4,000 miles an hour, without damaging the atmosphere in any way.

To put it in an environmental context, Space-ShipTwo is a real breakthrough. Every time the

NASA Shuttle launches, it has nearly the same negative environmental impact as the city of New York on a long holiday weekend. But SpaceShipTwo can carry either six people or the equivalent weight of payload into space for only the same CO_2 output as one business-class passenger from London to New York.

The secret is a launch from 50,000 feet, the light construction and the very simple method of re-entry, using a shuttlecock mechanism and then a simple glide back down to an existing runway. The simplicity of this project constantly reminds me of the natural human folly of creating very complex systems that end up justifying themselves and their existence – but end up stifling innovation.

NASA is a great organisation, but it has been hampered by the conflicting needs of government, politics and the military. Sometimes when you start from scratch with a clean sheet of paper, with the principle of keeping things simple, you get results that wouldn't be possible by leaving it to the so-called experts.

The project has also illustrated to me how we have become more and more reliant on government for technology development. The old idea from the seventeenth, eighteenth and nineteenth centuries, of offering prizes for the best developments in technology, rather got lost after the Second World War. For example, we would never have developed an accurate clock to find longitude without offering a prize. Ancient sailors used to navigate by the stars, the moon or to some extent, the sun – the sun would only tell them their latitude – but when there was extensive cloud cover, sailors quite literally became lost at sea. In 1714, the British Government offered £20,000 – a huge prize, the equivalent of about twenty million pounds today – for someone who could invent a way of showing longitude to within half a degree (two minutes of time). The methods would be tested on a ship, sailing from Great Britain to the West Indies. The Board of Longitude was set up to administer and judge the longitude prize. They received some bizarre suggestions, such as squaring the circle or inventing a perpetual motion machine, so many odd ideas that the phrase 'finding the longitude' became a sort of catchphrase for the pursuits of fools and lunatics. After several years of failure, people decided it was impossible. Then a clockmaker, John Harrison, invented a chronometer that worked. He went on to better it, with a small pocket watch, but had to fight to get the reward from a penny-pinching committee. Finally, at the age of 79, he appealed to King George III. The king was outraged, and said '[You] ... have been cruelly wronged. By God, Harrison, I will see you righted.'

Dava Sobel wrote the story in a best-selling book, *Longitude*, which I found fascinating. It became a methodology of how to develop new technology, with lots of prizes offered during the eighteenth and nineteenth centuries and into the twentieth. Most of the aircraft developed in those early years were winning prizes as well, which helped spur people on to great achievements. The *Daily Mail* prize for example, for the first flight across the Channel, was won by Louis Bleriot in 1909; and ten years later, Alcock and Brown won the Mail prize for crossing the Atlantic. Lindbergh was competing for a prize when he flew in the Spirit of St Louis, non-stop from

New York to Paris in 1927. The Spitfire was the result of the Schneider trophy, which was a series of prizes for technological development. All of this passion and enterprise and excitement got lost after World War Two, with the result that entrepreneurial inventors would have to be funded by governments to develop technology. Consequently, governments came to the forefront of new development and politics and budgetary considerations got in the way. Politics even got in the way of Britain's advanced satellite technology. We put the first satellite in space, long before Russia or America, and were on the brink of being the world leader in communications, but it was pulled for no apparent reason. Prime Minister Harold Wilson arbitrarily closed down Blue Streak, a long-range rocket; while it was Prime Minster Edward Heath who did the same with our Prospero space rocket that was already developed on the Isle of Wight. We even sold the Spitfire engine to the US for a million dollars immediately after World War Two and got left behind in the aero industry.

The X-prize is probably one of the first modern prizes developed since the war – and it's taught me a big lesson in how such prizes, outside of politics and bias, can spur individuals on to impossible heights of achievement. As a result, I've developed a $25 million prize to encourage technological development to fight climate change, that anyone can compete for and hopefully win.

The lesson I have learned throughout all this is that no goal is beyond our reach and even the impossible can become possible for those with vision and belief in themselves.

* * *

From spaceships to science fantasy comics might seem a wild jump; but in a way, they are very closely linked when one goes back to Dan Dare, Pilot of the Future. In all my business enterprises, I try to develop projects where the risk can be quantified and to some extent controlled. Sometimes, a project might not have an obvious profit in it, but what can be developed from it is more important. For example, *Student* wasn't profitable, but it led to Virgin Music, which was very profitable and which in turn funded the airline. Movies are another matter, and I have never really wanted to get involved with films because I can't quantify and control the risks.

However, in 2006, as soon as I saw the ideas for comics and animated films brought to me by Shekhar Kapur and Gotham Chopra, a film producer and the son of new age guru Deepak Chopra, I knew I wanted to get involved. The drawings and story-boards sizzled with creativity and energy. On the back of global movie and licensing deals, the market for comics and graphic novels worldwide is exploding. In the USA sales of graphic novels have grown by 44.7 per cent in the year to date. In the UK the market has doubled since 2003. Much of the growth in both territories has come from the emergence of comics out of Asia, born out of India's rich storytelling tradition. I could see them taking off fast, on a global level, and I set up Virgin Animation, to be run by Sharad Devarajan, and Virgin Comics, with Chopra and Kapur. To start with, we will focus primarily on the Asian market and will be based in Bangalore, India's hi-tech centre, and in New York City.

Film director John Woo, maker of beautiful, balletic action films, is creating a comic book series for us and we intend to work with the world's greatest storytellers, both famous and first-timers, through our Maverick and Director's Cut lines, which are specifically intended to attract innovative thinkers and artists to comics and provide them with a platform to create their stories in a medium akin to a movie with an unlimited budget. Nicolas Cage, Guy Ritchie and Dave Stewart, the former Eurythmics star, have been signed to turn movie ideas into comic books. None of these three has ever been involved in a project like this before and asking for their participation is an example of Virgin's innovative thinking.

I believe that in the next decade India, with its 600 million teenagers alone, will become one of the largest producers, as well as the largest consumers, of entertainment products, from fantasy comics, films, animation, toys, video games and a whole range of linked consumer products. I want to be in on the ground floor, tapping into innovative concepts from around the world, giving a whole generation of young, creative thinkers a voice.

From all this, I have learned a couple of lessons. Be adaptable enough to move fast when you have to – though in this context, 'fast' is a matter of degree. Sometimes it's a good idea to have ideas on the back burner and wait for the developments to come around, as I did with Virgin Galactic, and then pounce on them as quickly as you can. And also, keep things simple. People get lost when a systematic approach becomes over complex and they lose sight of the actual goal.

I haven't moved away from having a bit of fun, though, and if fun can be combined with promotion, that's all well and good. I have a cameo role in the latest Bond movie, *Casino Royale*, alongside a Virgin Galactic plane; and in the new *Superman* (alongside a Virgin Galactic spacecraft). The producers said they wanted to bring Superman into the modern era using Virgin rather than NASA; I thought he was always in the future. It's where I've always been heading.

14. THINK YOUNG

You've got to challenge the big ones
Keep it casual
Haggle: everything is negotiable
Have fun working
Do the right things for the brand
Smile for the cameras!
Don't lead 'sheep', herd 'cats'
Move like a bullet
Small is beautiful
Be a common, regular person

Above are my top ten tips, which I listed in a talk I gave to students at a business school. I believe that whatever your age, a fresh and youthful approach in everything, from business to lifestyle, will renew and re-energise. I always say, train for the future and think global. If something works in one country, it can work in another. Don't stumble on, but build on, cultural differences.

All these aphorisms are different ways of saying the same thing: 'Think young' and by that, I don't mean you have to be young, or that you're over the hill at thirty. People who stop thinking and feeling young tend to be rigid in their approach to life and that's not what creativity, growth, personal development is all about.

The one man in the world I admire and respect above all others is Nelson Mandela. Having spent 18 of his 27 years in prison breaking rocks on Robben Island didn't break his spirit. As he walked down the dusty road from the prison to the boat that was to take him to freedom, he said he realised that if he allowed bitterness to take him over, he would never really be free. During that walk, he forgave his oppressors because if he hadn't they would have finally destroyed him. At that moment, he truly became free – and that was what made him great.

When President Bill Clinton was going through a tough personal time, played out in the public glare, Mandela said to him: 'They destroyed my marriage. They abused me physically and mentally. They could take everything except my mind and heart. Those things I would have to give away and I decided not to give them away.' And then Mandela added, 'Neither should you.'

I first made contact with Mandela in 1988 through Peter Gabriel, one of my closest friends, who organised the Free Nelson Mandela concerts as part of a wider international campaign run by Amnesty International. Although those concerts raised awareness enormously of the injustice he was suffering, he wasn't freed for another two years, in 1990. Generally, when you meet a hero, you are disappointed. My impression of Nelson Mandela was enhanced when we finally met. Our friendship developed and

I learned to call him Madiba, an honorary title given to elders in his tribe. I admired all he was achieving in the new South Africa, and worldwide, with his philosophy of Peace and Reconciliation.

Important lessons can be learned by studying my experiences in South Africa. It is a crucible of youth and energy, a melting pot of original ideas, and things that work there do so faster than in many other places because of this urge to progress. For this reason, entrepreneurs, business people, health professionals and educators might benefit by studying the South African model.

I was to be in South Africa on numerous occasions from the 1990s – for example, when Virgin Atlantic opened a route to Cape Town in 1999. My growing love for the country led to my acquiring Ulusaba, a game reserve in the Sabi Sands region near the Kruger National Park, a place that has given me and my family a great deal of pleasure. It was through Mandela that I became aware of the great work being done among young people through a newly formed university campus, known as CIDA – Community and Individual Development Association. It is an inner-city university in Johannesburg for underprivileged African youth, almost totally subsidised by donors. My ears pricked up when I heard the vision behind the university was to offer one central accredited degree – Business – which could be used anywhere, and which would encourage a sense of entrepreneurship. In addition, there are many extra curricula activities, including African dance, martial arts, TM meditation, sports and gardening. I can remember gaining a sense of excitement as I sat before an audience with Mandela during a visit by the Dalai Lama, discussing such topics with the bright and eager students as the gap between rich and poor, race and religion and even the benefit of meditation and education. I was pleased to be able to put the Dalai Lama and Mandela together after that discussion. Previously, the president of South Africa hadn't allowed them to meet.

It has been commented upon that I dropped out of school early and even Bill Gates dropped out of Harvard. However, this isn't necessarily the best example to follow. I think that an education – preferably to university level – helps people to help themselves. It is something I'm really passionate about, particularly in South Africa, a nation that's important as a beacon in the undeveloped world. Education gives young people a chance to get themselves economic freedom. One man who shines above all others in the field of education is Taddy Bletcher. Almost single-handedly, he launched Africa's first free university in downtown Johannesburg.

University education in South Africa is expensive and applications are competitive. Poor children from the townships or rural communities have never stood a chance to get their feet on the first rung. Taddy's vision was to start a university that cost less than R4,000 (£284.75) to study for a degree, including books and administration. CIDA started from ground zero, which meant they had to be creative in coming up with solutions. Companies like KPMG were approached for volunteers to teach accounting. In turn, the students were taken on as interns by the companies. All students are expected to give back, and this includes taking turns to clean and cook and, more importantly, to teach in their home communities. Another brilliantly innovative idea is that as soon as they start earning, they are expected to sponsor another student from their community through university.

As Taddy says, 'When you look back on your deathbed one day and ask, "Was it all worth it?" I'll be able to say, every day would have made it worth it.'

Young people in Africa are desperate to gain an education, so much so that one or two of them have hitchhiked 1,500 miles to get to CIDA. I wish young people in the UK who truant and drop out of school could see this for themselves. In order to reach those who are too far away from any chance of getting to college, we are discussing setting up an international travelling university in tented campuses. In turn it will go to different countries and teach conflict resolution and dealing with social issues. For one term it will set up in Palestine; another term in Sierra Leone; another term in Somalia; another term in Ethiopia and so on. One idea copied from CIDA is that those who gain an education will then go on to act as teachers and mentors to others and the benefits will expand.

Human capital is the most costly of all factors in any operating business. Times have changed globally, but I spend a lot of time and effort in South Africa, where their unique multicultural young society makes it a good place to use as a pilot platform to try out new ideas. I believe that increasing entrepreneurship there is the golden highway to economic freedom, and this is why I established the Branson School of Entrepreneurship in the CIDA campus. Coincidentally, it opened its doors in the very bank building in which Mandela worked as a young man before he was imprisoned. All the tuition is directed towards enabling young people to launch their own businesses. So far we have 300 students, about 30 of whom are developing small businesses – we call it incubating – that we'll help support for 12–18 months.

The Institute for Public Policy Research (IPPR) in the United States examined a programme where financial education has been compulsory in some areas since 1957. Their research shows that children who attend lessons in personal finance and household budgeting could be up to £32,000 richer by the time they reach their forties than their peers who didn't receive the lessons. Financially educated children went on to save around 1.5 per cent more of their income each year. I recognise that, despite my own example, there is nothing wrong with a formal education as long as you don't let it stunt you.

When people ask me what business they can get into, I always tell them the same thing: whatever business you choose to get into, have a passion for what you do, for the moment it becomes all about the money is the moment you will cease to go forward. I tell them to worry about survival rather than sorting out the world's problems for the first few years. If capitalism is to be given a good name, then essentially capitalists need to give back to society. At the beginning of this chapter I wrote: 'Don't lead sheep, herd cats.' It's easy to herd sheep, but impossible to lead them from the front. Cats, on the other hand, are independent and intelligent and those are the kind of people we want to employ at Virgin. A good lesson to take onboard for anyone in business is to employ thinkers, not yes men. There's a danger that people become concerned and fearful of taking risks. Perhaps they have a partner or a mortgage which prevents them. They must not let this constrict them in being bold and being brave. I was fifteen and had no ties, no strings and nothing to lose. But those with something to lose might consider that by aiming high, they might achieve a lot more.

I have always found that many of my best ideas for starting new businesses, or expanding them into new areas, come from either conversations with people, or from overhearing something almost in passing. The true entrepreneur will never have his antennae in 'switched off' mode. A case in point is how I came to buy a chain of health clubs in South Africa. Because of my interest in physical fitness, in 1999 I had already launched Virgin Active, a group of health clubs in the UK, which later expanded into Spain, Italy, Portugal and Namibia. But I wasn't aware that Mandela knew of this connection until 2001. One day, while I was lying in the bathtub, I got a call from him.

'Richard, we have a chain of some eighty health clubs here in South Africa that is about to be liquidated,' he said. 'It would be a great blow if this were to happen, because these clubs were set up through a black empowerment scheme, and thousands of jobs would be lost. Is there anything you can do?'

'Leave it with me, I'll see what can be done,' I said.

I flew to South Africa the next day and after I'd looked at the situation, I thought that we could rescue these clubs by injecting some capital and putting them on a sound business footing. Ultimately, Virgin Active's South African operation proved to be the most successful in the group. South Africans are very keen on training and our clubs have more members than those in other countries and they visit the clubs more frequently. Some of the clubs average 3,000 people a day. The membership is both black and white – about 20 per cent black at the moment – but the proportions will level out because the emerging black middle class is the fastest growing segment.

We have 20 new clubs opening shortly, and it seems an indication of the remarkable turnaround that some of these will be established in the heart of townships like Soweto. I can remember when people were very pessimistic about the future of such places.

We are also helping local black entrepreneurs to develop their brands in health club and sporting activity markets, partly by passing on thousands of pieces of equipment to fledgling clubs each time we update. Obesity and diabetes are on the increase in developed countries, and this trend is now on the increase in Africa and to help combat this we have started children's sections for the 125,000 children who come into our clubs with their parents. We are supported by some medical aid companies, which offer their members subsidised membership and we have programmes to recruit, train and develop staff. So far, we have recruited 20 young black graduates just out of CIDA, who will be fast-tracked for development for management positions at the clubs. We are also known as a company that is starting to take on ex-prisoners and heroin addicts. Working with the South African government, we believe in using affirmative action when it comes to anyone who needs extra help. I don't think it should be decided just on colour, but also on people who have been sent to prison. When they come out, unless they get a job they might re-offend and society will be harmed in the meantime. If Capitalism is to be given a good name it must give back to society.

I believe that anything can be turned around if the people are empowered. The same applies to families, as well as to businesses. People react to the way in which they are treated. The fact that youngsters in the UK have got such a bad reputation in the media, to such an extent that they're now perceived as the 'worst' in Europe can't only be their fault. Virgin Unite is all about uniting the 50,000 or so people who work for Virgin in whatever capacity – and that includes me – to work together as a team and drive entrepreneurial approaches to social and environmental issues and so we see first hand, through people like Camila Batmanghelidjh, what's going on at a grassroots level.

Camila set up Kids Company in a deprived area of South London to support some 11,000 of the most chronically deprived young people who have severe behavioural, emotional and social difficulties resulting from childhood trauma and neglect. Through listening to people like her, I have come to believe that the breakdown in family life has played a big role in lack of social cohesion and skills. Even a simple thing, like sitting down to meals at a table and conversing, as my parents did with my sisters and me as children, can be a major turning point.

Children need adults to teach and guide them, exactly as in the wild with fox cubs or lions. I think of my own mother who used to say, 'Ricky, don't just roll about doing nothing.' My generation simply didn't loll about, watching television and playing video games. The interaction between adults and children was very strong. They guided; we followed.

Today's rootless children who learn only from their peers are lost to society. Parents need to share responsibility, not wait for the government to come up with solutions. Young people have a huge amount of energy and potential to do good and none of them should be written off. They are the future. It will be up to them to solve the problems, such as pollution, depleting fish stocks, the destruction of the natural world, existing diseases or new plagues like AIDS, that their predecessors haven't solved, or, in many cases, caused.

The undeveloped world, particularly Africa, has big problems that needn't exist and this, I think, is where business people can help to solve problems in different ways than charity workers. Each group has a vital role, but they are different. Charity workers have to deal with what *is* and try to help in the field, but businessmen and entrepreneurs can help solve the problems on a wider scale, through funding and science.

In Africa about one and a half million children and about 750,000 pregnant women die from malaria every year. They die because they're bitten by mosquitoes. So how do you stop the mosquitoes biting them? It seems unbelievable that there is no concerted campaign throughout Africa to deal with the mosquito problem, yet the answer is very simple.

If every single person in Africa had a mosquito net impregnated with a substance which would kill the mosquitoes, and if the walls of their homes were painted with a similar substance, the problem could be solved. It's a solution that's not beyond our capability, yet it hasn't been done.

HIV/AIDS is another disease which should have been dealt with by now. So far HIV/AIDS has killed 17 million people in Africa, and about 30 million more are sufferers. This is preposterous in this day and age. I remember the first time I went to a hospital in Africa and saw rows and rows and rows of people dying of AIDS. The average ward in any one morning had six empty beds from the people who had died the night before. It was both terrifying and unbelievable. Now Virgin Unite is in talks with the United Nations and other people about setting up a fast response Operations Centre that can co-ordinate all the humanitarian activities that are taking place in Africa. If, for example, something works in Nigeria we can push more resources into it. If things are not working elsewhere we can move resources there. All it will take is the will, initiative, and money. We need people who think big, not resignation and hand wringing.

At the beginning of 2006 the Pentagon was voted $125 billion a year over ten years to pay for the war in Iraq. To compare, the annual cost of raising African health to world standards ($25–$35 billion); educating every child in the world ($7 billion); clean water and sanitation worldwide ($9 billion); dealing with HIV/Aids worldwide ($10 billion) would leave change from $65 billion. Put into perspective, does making war make sense?

I was in Johannesburg in late 2003 when Mandela addressed the press in the run up to '46664', a benefit concert for HIV/AIDS which we helped organise, along with Peter Gabriel and Brian May (of Queen). He spoke briefly, and to the point:

'AIDS is a tragedy of unprecedented proportions unfolding in Africa. No longer is AIDS just a disease; it is a human rights issue. For the sake of the world, we must act now to raise funds to help those affected by AIDS and raise awareness to help to prevent further spread of HIV. "46664" was my prison number for eighteen years when I was in prison on Robben Island. I was known as just a number. Millions of people today infected with AIDS are just that, a number. They too are serving a prison sentence for life, that is why for the first time I am allowing my prison number, 46664, to brand this campaign.'

Sitting next to him during the concert with his wonderful wife, Graca Machel, with Joan and Holly, while listening to Peter Gabriel sing, was one of the most moving experiences of my life.

I thought I had a youthful approach to life, even in my fifties; but in his eighties, Mandela seems to be compensating for all those years in prison by his vision and passion for life. I have already written in an earlier chapter about how I gained the help of King Hussein of Jordan and Sir Edward Heath to negotiate with Saddam Hussein and fly into Iraq to bring home 43 injured and sick hostages before the first conflict in 1990; but I never expected to be involved in the same arena again. But by 2003, in the wake of September 11, as the crisis deepened in Iraq it looked as if Bush would go to war. I was opposed to the invasion plans, because I thought it was perhaps the worst foreign policy decision since Suez. You shouldn't have to kill or maim thousands of people to get rid of one individual. I believed if they could offer Saddam an escape route, bloodshed would be avoided. I kept thinking you have to give somebody like Saddam a way out otherwise he's like a cornered animal – they have to fight. And perhaps to some extent, Saddam didn't really believe they would invade.

The picture was confused and growing more urgent by the moment. I thought the only person who could persuade him to step down as president and go to live in exile was Mandela. I telephoned him, then followed up with a simple letter.

Dear Madiba,
As always it was very good to talk to you. I thought I'd send you a very brief note setting out our discussion.

America and Britain have definitely decided to go to war. Inevitably there will be many civilian casualties.

I believe there may be only one way to stop a war in Iraq and I believe you may be the only person in the world to achieve it.

If Saddam Hussein could be persuaded to retire to Libya (or somewhere else), with full immunity, I do not believe it would be possible for America to press ahead with the war. If he were to make this sacrifice to avoid his people going through yet more suffering he would enhance his reputation considerably. The personal alternative will be the fate of Noriega, Milosevic or worse.

Knowing your relationship with President Qaddafi and the respect you are held in in Iraq you are perhaps the only person who could organise this.

I believe you would have the credibility to persuade Saddam Hussein to step down. By flying out with you – to say, Libya – he could leave with his head held high. It would be the best thing he could do for his people.

If it helps you I would be happy to send you a plane to take you there and back (hopefully via Libya!)

I'll talk to you once you've spoken with Thabo [Mbeki, the president of South Africa]. Kind regards as always, Richard

The plan was for Mandela to go to Baghdad, talk to Saddam, then they would fly out together. This would assure Saddam that he would be safe. But before we did anything, Mandela wanted us to get Kofi Annan's blessing. Kofi Annan was initially cautious about the idea and was worried Mandela would be taken hostage by Saddam. And perhaps to some extent Saddam didn't believe in the proposal. I spoke to Kofi Annan and eventually he was convinced that it was a good plan and gave us the go-ahead. The most amazing thing about it was that Mandela was prepared to give it a go because, at his age, he thought he was expendable. I told Mandela that I would go along with him if it would help. I wasn't worried about my own safety – as I said to Mandela, I have done many dangerous things – but the decision was being left up to him.

Four Virgin executives, including Will Whitehorn, were given secret instructions to help make the peace plan a success and they arranged for a private jet to be standing by in Johannesburg from 17 March to fly to Iraq. Two days later, as we were on the brink of going, the bombing started and coalition forces invaded Iraq. I will never know what might have happened had the invasion been delayed by a couple more days. The whole history of the war and the Middle East might have been different.

The invasion of Iraq and all that has happened since, there and elsewhere in the world, inspired me to set up a group of non-political figures called The Elders to help avert future conflicts. It's in its infancy but Mandela has agreed to be the founding father. This is something that came as an idea between me, Peter Gabriel and Mandela. We talked it through and felt there was a gap in the world, where there's lots of leadership through military and economic and political power but not a lot of leadership based on wisdom for the global village today. We've been working on it in the background for the last couple of years.

I was in South Africa recently with Jean Oelwang, our globetrotting managing director of Virgin Unite, and was very encouraged by the progress of the wide range of entrepreneurial social projects we are developing. I try to be hands on as much as possible. For example, a while back, when I saw that some of our staff were HIV positive but didn't have anywhere to go to get entroviral drugs, we donated a clinic in Lesotho for about 100,000 people in the surrounding area. As encouragement, Joan and I went along and publically got tested in front of all our staff. I'm also very passionate and hands on with various environmental projects, because Africa is so vulnerable to global warming. It bears the brunt of many of the careless activities that have taken place, and are still happening, in the rest of the world – but Africans themselves can also play their part, such as replacing paraffin with biofuel, which is much safer and cleaner. Once the women (who do the cooking) in the townships realise this, they want to make the change, but initially, we have to help them financially and by example.

Mandela summed it up well in his 1994 inaugural speech when he was elected president of South Africa: 'Our deepest fear is not that we are inadequate, our greatest fear is that we are powerful beyond measure. It is our light not our darkness that most frightens us. We ask ourselves, who am I to be fabulous, brilliant, talented, gorgeous? Actually, who are you not to be, you are a child of God and your playing small does not serve the world. There is nothing enlightened about shrinking so that other people won't feel insecure around you. We are all meant to shine, like children do. We are born to make manifest the glory of God within us. It is not just in some of us; it is in every one of us. And as we let our own light shine, we unconsciously give people permission to do the same. As we are liberated by our fears, our presence automatically liberates others.'

They are stirring words, containing lessons we can all embrace. I have certainly learned from them.

EPILOGUE

I have always lived my life by thriving on opportunity and adventure. The motive that drives me has always been to set myself challenges and try to achieve them. Every lesson I have learned has been as a direct result of these tests. They include:

Just do it
Think yes, not no
Challenge yourself
Have goals
Have fun
Make a difference
Stand on your own feet
Be loyal
Live life to the full
Nothing ventured, nothing gained

My favourite time of the day is evening, at Necker, seated around a big, happy table, with my family and friends, having fun. This paradise island combines many of my dreams and aims in life. When Joan and I first found the island, buying it became a goal. Raising the money and building a house on it, then getting water in, were huge challenges to be solved. I never once said, 'can't'. I went for it, and I did it. Today, it's a place where my family and friends and I have a lot of fun. It's where I relax and think – and some of my best ideas come out of the blue. I have to keep an open mind to see their virtue.

Something occurred recently, which seems to sum up what I'm about and how I view life. It was when a hurricane blew across the Virgin Islands. My home, the Great House on Necker, is built of natural materials, mainly wood, and might appear to be quite fragile – but it was built to withstand winds of 180 miles an hour. However, I didn't take refuge indoors. Hurricanes only come to Necker about once every fifty years, and I hate the idea of not experiencing something – especially an event as rare and dramatic as that. Being out there in the storm was a rare opportunity, so I got into the swimming pool and kept my head down as the winds raged overhead. It was a completely awesome experience, watching the seas crash over the reef, feeling the velocity of the wind, hearing the incredible noise. Weathering the storm was fantastic – and that is what my life is like. Being out there in a hurricane, and surviving.

Growing older hasn't changed me. When I develop a new idea, as soon as it's going well, I want to push the boat out again. Joan keeps saying, 'Why? You're getting on for sixty, Richard. Take it easy. Let's enjoy it.' But I've lived by the dangerous – and sometimes rather foolish – maxim that I'm prepared to try anything once. I'm driven by new challenges. One is transforming Britain's rail system from being the worst in the world to the best. Recently, we took delivery of 900 state-of-the-art environmentally friendly new trains and they went into service. I believe that if you can do a few things like that, at the end of the day, you can say you've lived a good life. If I put all my money in the bank and retire in the Caribbean, I think it would be a waste of my unique position, where I can make huge changes for the better. I want to keep renewing myself and the opportunities I have. It's like sex. It's as satisfying at fifty as it is at twenty, but nothing can beat that first time. Incidentally, the best advice I got from my dad was, 'Wear a condom'!

I spend a third of my time promoting, a third on new ventures and a third on fighting fires. I would like my legacy to have created one of the most respected companies in the world. Not necessarily the biggest. People ask me at what point in my life do I feel a success? The answer is, I hope I will never be complacent. I'm still nervous about public speaking, for example, and there are moments when I have doubts over many things. But about ten or twenty years ago, once I felt that Virgin was financially secure, I decided that I could be more than just a money-making machine, running companies. At Virgin we're lucky in that we've always approached business in a different way, by focusing on our people and our customers, and by allowing our businesses to have autonomy. If you look for the best in your employees, they'll flourish. If you criticise or look for the worst, they'll shrivel up. We all need lots of watering. We have a really wonderful team of people and I feel that whatever happens, Virgin will be in safe hands – which leaves me more time to think of other things.

I feel it's important to try to leave the world a better place. For every commercial idea I have, I want to develop an idea which I hope will do some good, such as Virgin Unite. VU is intended as a way of getting all the Virgin staff around the world to work together to help with tough social challenges. I hope we can make a difference. I think the biggest challenge of all isn't facing me alone. It's facing mankind – and it's global warming. That rare hurricane that I experienced for fun could become the norm. Places that have never known extremes of weather could suddenly find that great winds, fierce heat, drought, huge rainstorms and floods are everyday events. It won't be fun. When facing the carnage after the events of 9/11 in New York, Al Gore said, 'It's the end of fun.' Well, I want us to continue to have fun, and the only way for us to do this is to take global warming and climate change seriously.

I still believe in all my mother's challenges, but we applied them to a lesser degree with Holly and Sam. Joan is a very down-to-earth Scottish woman. She made sure that we were always surrounded by other family members and living an everyday life. Children have the most fantastic binding effect on a relationship. Obviously, there are downs in a relationship. But for me, it just keeps getting stronger and stronger and stronger. Love really does grow. We live a very stable, normal life and as a result, Holly and Sam are extremely well balanced. They live in the modern world, but like me they were brought up to challenge themselves. I encouraged them but never pushed them. I am very proud that Holly decided to become a paediatrician. She has passed her exams and currently is doing her houseman year at a big London hospital. Recently, she delivered her first baby, a key moment in her training.

I am really proud of Sam, who is very creative, playing music and challenging himself to a crossing of the Arctic (with his dad!).

All the things in this book are my lessons and my goals in life, the things I believe in. But they are not unique to me. Everyone needs to keep learning. Everyone needs goals. Each and every one of my lessons can be applied to all of us. Whatever we want to be, whatever we want to do, we can do it, because we can. Go ahead, take that first step – just do it. The best of luck to you, and have fun along the way.

INDEX